DINNER AT OMAR KHAYYAM'S

George M. Mardikian

TO MY FRIENDS

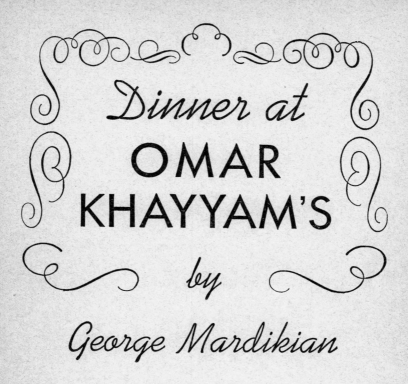

Dinner at OMAR KHAYYAM'S

by

George Mardikian

HOOPER PUBLISHING COMPANY · SAN FRANCISCO

SECOND PRINTING DECEMBER 1944
THIRD PRINTING NOVEMBER 1945
FOURTH PRINTING MARCH 1948
FIFTH PRINTING APRIL 1949
SIXTH PRINTING APRIL 1952
SEVENTH PRINTING JUNE 1955
EIGHTH PRINTING DECEMBER 1957
NINTH PRINTING JUNE 1960
TENTH PRINTING JUNE 1961
ELEVENTH PRINTING MARCH 1963
TWELFTH PRINTING MARCH 1966

PRINTED AND BOUND IN U. S. A. BY HOOPER PRINTING & LITHOGRAPH CO.

CONTENTS

Contents

FOREWORD

BY WILLIAM SAROYAN

WHEN George Mardikian told me he was thinking of writing a cookbook, I knew it would be the most original one ever written, so I told him to be sure to go to work right away. I have never found it possible not to encourage any man who feels he has a book to write, let alone a great man like George. "Get that big frame of yours out of that kitchen," I told him, "and start writing." Now the book is written and I have given it the once over. Just as I thought, it is a prize package of a book, but it is *more* than a cookbook. It is the smiling chef himself—the generous-hearted, enthusiastic, easygoing George Mardikian himself talking to you just as he does in his famous restaurant, Omar Khayyam's; it is the big man with the bright face coming over to your table with a half dozen out-of-the-world dishes and telling you how they happened to come about in the great fable of man and hunger. It is the historian telling you history mingled skillfully with anecdotes from George's own beautiful fable. It is the comedian laughing with delight at the story of how he outwitted famine by inventing fabulous dishes from such lowly and abundant things as grain, water, salt, imagination and poetry. It is the man himself telling everybody how wonderful it is to be alive, and especially how wonderful it is to be alive in America. Naturally, I am delighted about George's book, just as I am always delighted with the food he serves and the manner in which he serves it. George Mardikian is the rarest chef in America—a man of exquisite good health, which spreads itself all around his restaurant like light from a walking human sun; a delightful wit with more stories than Omar him-

I

self; a continuous searcher for more and better table delights; a wise companion; and an eloquent speaker of both English and Armenian—my two favorite languages.

George is a countryman of mine, but that is not the only reason I am so fond of him—there are many countrymen of mine whom I find it most difficult to cherish. I am fond of George because he is one of the most civilized human beings I have ever encountered. Because he has always been infinitely more than a guy in a kitchen preparing a supper for his friends and himself. Because he has never found it necessary to fuss too strenuously with the dull matters of making a profit and paying rent. Because his intention to make of his restaurants a civilized atmosphere for civilized people of all kinds has been more than realized. And because, in spite of all the demands on his time, he has never allowed himself to give anyone, however great or humble, the impression of being too busy to sit around and loaf. He is an excellent poker player and I have yet to see him lose without grace. He is interested in all good things and has yet to let a writer or a painter or a composer out of his restaurant without stuffing him with every kind of wonderful food in the place. On the other hand, he insists on feeding the lowly—he banquets newsboys as if they were the children of kings, and he fills his restaurant with homeless men as if they were the greatest men of our time.

I would like to tell you more about this remarkable man—but here is his book. I believe that anybody who owns this book is going to learn to make a good many dishes on his own in his own kitchen; that he is going to appreciate good food more than ever; and that he is going to get more out of the experience of living.

San Francisco, California.

INTRODUCTION

BY JOSEPH HENRY JACKSON

When George Mardikian came to San Francisco to open his famous restaurant, Omar Khayyam's, he was well aware that he followed an ancient and honorable tradition.

You will discover early in this book that George began by knowing a great deal about the cookery of the Middle East. You will learn that he broadened this base as he went along, studying the tastes of Europe and of Africa, learning what well-to-do Americans on luxury cruises enjoyed in the way of food, finally coming to this country to study American cookery at its source. You will see—you can't help seeing—that George's interest in his fellow-man's appetite is keen, that his understanding of gastronomy is profound.

Yet even the specialist might know all these things, might have all of the Mardikian sensitiveness in culinary matters, and still remain unaware that in California, and in San Francisco particularly, there has developed a very special regard for food and for the man who knows how to prepare it. The truth is that San Franciscans have always been sympathetic to what Arthur Machen once called "the great art of eating and drinking." And for many reasons George Mardikian knew this well before he so much as opened the doors of his San Francisco Omar Khayyam's. He had thought about it, for one thing. He had learned it at first hand, through working in San Francisco restaurants long before opening his earlier Omar Khayyam's in Fresno, two hundred miles to the south. Best of all, George had taken pains to study the record, to examine the growth of American cookery in general and most especially California's—

and San Francisco's—contributions to the tradition. He knew what he was about, and from their first taste of a dinner at Omar's, San Franciscans knew he knew. George Mardikian had realized the significant truth that the San Francisco palate will invariably respond to a new and pleasant sensation, that the San Franciscan's taste is catholic and that he, George, had something to offer which would gratify a connoisseurship as well trained as any American's anywhere. Wherefore Omar Khayyam's, and this book that has come out of it.

From the beginning, America's cookery has been enriched and ornamented from the culinary storehouse of the rest of the world. In colonial Virginia the housewife made her cakes, her pies and tarts, from the recipes in her English mother's or grand-mother's cookbook. It was the greatest of all philosophers in the field of food and drink, a political refugee from his native France a century and a half ago, who taught Boston's finest chef how to broil eggs with cheese. Even the turkey, bird of the Western Hemisphere though it is, depends for its holiday succulence upon stuffings which, in their fanciful variety, derive from half a dozen countries of Europe and Asia. If, out of this admirable eclecticism, American cooking does not develop into the noblest form of the art yet known, it will not be the fault of the experts who have brought us the fruits of their experience and their taste.

The chances are that no city anywhere understands this better than San Francisco.

When the S.S. *California* stood through the Golden Gate on that raw February morning almost a century ago, the first Forty-Niners that jammed her decks may well have felt their hearts sink as they saw the town to which they had come. This was no Boston or New York, no Philadelphia or Baltimore. Wet, cold, flea-ridden from the moment they set foot on shore, those early Argonauts staggered on their sea-legs through the mud to whatever crude board-and-canvas lodging they could find and wished with all their hearts they had never come. Then they discovered that this haphazard, jerry-built San Francisco had restaurants. They thought of their stomachs, shrunken and tender from ship-rations of maggoty beef and moldy bread, and they loosened their belts and set to. It took no more than their first meal to make them Californians and above all San Franciscans. When it came to food and drink, this, their new dwelling-place, was no mean city.

What these newcomers could not have known was that the *Californio*, their predecessor in this land of gold, had always been fussy about his dinner.

To be sure, California was a province and life was therefore provincial. The *ranchero* might run his cattle on a hundred leagues of land yet have to nudge a pig out of the way before walking in at his own front door. That was life in the provinces. But California grew fine grapes and the *padres* had labored in their vineyards and wineries for many years. When a man could pasture cattle and sheep by the tens of thousands, the finest of veal and beef and lamb were his for the trouble of slaughtering. Antelope swarmed in the region of the Bay. Over the Valley lakes, the geese and ducks darkened the sky in season. Fat quail scurried underfoot in all the little canyons of the Coast Range, and enormous salmon spawned in the rivers. If a man wanted something special, say a hindquarter of young elk or a tender bear's paw spiced and baked, there was no real difficulty about getting it. The Californian of the gracious forties ate and drank with gusto. He and his friends were *caballeros* and nothing was too good for them.

Moreover, the Californian was a man of discrimination; he knew how his food should be prepared and he saw to it that it was done that way. Down in Monterey or out on a back country *rancho* the vegetable garden was as important as the bed of Castile roses whose slips had been so carefully cherished through all the long journey up from Mexico City. And no garden patch was complete without its clusters of herbs—basil and thyme, rosemary, marjoram and sage, fennel and coriander, even the pungent, mint-like *yerba buena* for which San Francisco was first named. When the *ranchero* sat down to his morning chocolate it was no watery-sweet cocoa. The Indian maids had been taught to make it as it was drunk in Mexico, a well-whipped, frothy draught in which the chocolate and sugar and milk in due proportions had been smoothed and enriched and mellowed by the addition of a beaten egg, a flavoring of vanilla and a pinch of cinnamon. The Indian had contributed his bit of knowledge, too; from him the Spanish colonial had learned the uses of the delicate pine nut, and its sweet and crunchy meats were added to the traditional citron that made the *pan dulce* what it was. No doubt about it, the Californian of early days had known how to pamper his palate. Now, with the golden flood pouring down from the foothills and San Francisco filled with men who had money to pay for whatever notion came into their heads, food and drink in the best Spanish Californian style formed the foundation of the city's surprisingly fine cuisine. The Forty-Niners were astonished but happy.

The fifties saw San Francisco grow like magic. What if devastating fires did wipe out the city time and again? The oceans of the world were white with the sails of ships bringing to this newest and richest metropolis the luxuries it demanded. The clippers were ballasted with good eastern bricks, even sandstone, and as fast as the ashes cooled, San Francisco was rebuilt in good, solid masonry. Perhaps there was little time to waste in laying out broad avenues; San Francisco was still a man's city, with little thought of the family mansions that would come later. There would be time enough to build homes. Meanwhile the ships brought cooks, and San Francisco's taste in food and drink burgeoned in a dozen directions at once.

As early as 1851, the San Franciscan could drink at solid mahogany and watch himself tilt his glass in a mirror longer than he had ever seen at home. He might eat from the finest porcelain under crystal chandeliers, at a table draped with snowy linen. What gold could buy was his; the ships brought it from the ends of the earth. Barreled oysters and the rarest French wines were commonplace. Miner or man of business might lunch at Clayton's on the specialty of the house—a broiled quail and a glass of punch. At Winn's Fountain Head or The Branch he could choose between an oyster stew with brown bread and ale, or a slice of cold boiled salmon mayonnaise, cut before his eyes from the giant fish and served with a superior *Sauternes* at four dollars a bottle. By the middle fifties, it was possible in San Francisco to take your choice of the whole world's cookery—French, German, Spanish, Chinese, Italian, whatever you liked. If you longed for a *bouillabaisse* the Bay teemed with fish, and the French restaurateurs imported their saffron as a matter of course. Buckwheat was grown in California now, and the San Franciscan who cherished a taste for the tiny Dutch pancakes drenched in melted butter and powdered sugar had only to choose his restaurant. Pepper, mace, and nutmeg came in the holds of clippers bringing the best China tea and shark's fins for the little yellow men who were industriously working over the mine-dumps of the careless Americans, and planting bamboo and beans for the tender sprouts that were such good eating. As for game, there were curlew, plover, and snipe in abundance. Hams, imported from Westphalia or home cured, were served with champagne sauce, and if you liked your sautéed kidneys with a dash of Madeira the chef at the Tehama House would be delighted to oblige. As for liquid refreshment, the first St. Francis Hotel, on Clay

Street near the water front, offered a select list, with a good Medoc at four dollars, London Dock Port at five, assorted liqueurs at fifty cents a glass, and even an 1820 brandy at six dollars a bottle. Sprawling and rough still, dusty in summer and knee-deep in mud in the winter, its sidewalks of planking and its plumbing of the sketchiest, San Francisco nevertheless knew the importance of good food, paid for the best and saw that it got it.

The city's tradition in food was thus set and shaped from the beginning. A town thronged with men who had no homes had encouraged fine restaurants out of necessity. Now it continued the pattern and developed it as a matter of pride.

When the gold rush was followed by the great silver stream from the Comstock, San Francisco grew richer than ever. By the end of the sixties, the railroad and telegraph had linked Pacific and Atlantic, and it was merely a question of decent self-respect to show the eastern banker, the railroad man, the politician, the Civil War general, that San Francisco could and would give him a banquet or a breakfast better than he could get at home. Silver overlapped the land-and-wheat booms, and the profits funneled through the city. So did the wealth produced by the suddenly expanded shipping industry. The seventies and eighties were still bonanza days in spite of recurrent money panics. San Francisco was the City Where Anything Could Happen, the carefree, sparkling, romantic, energetic city it had been from the first. Its citizens, having replaced red flannel shirts with fine linen and black broadcloth, sent their sons back to Harvard or Yale or Princeton and afterward gave them the Grand Tour; gloved and glossy on Paris boulevards, these young men of the world spoke with nostalgia of San Francisco's Maison Dorée, of the Poodle Dog and of Marchand's whose alcoves were so discreetly curtained and whose proprietor delicately let it be known that private rooms were available for *tête-à-tête* suppers and that service might be had at any hour of the day or night. San Francisco was youthful, daring, brash; its people frankly boasted that they had the best—in the theater, in music, in the restaurants that made life civilized, frontier or no frontier. In what other city, they liked to ask, might one find a Cliff House, in whose broadly glassed breakfast room of a Sunday morning one might survey the blue Pacific and consume cold breast of young turkey served with a slice of broiled Smithfield ham and corn fritters? And had not the famous dish, Oysters Kirkpatrick, originated in San Francisco? It had, in the kitchen of the Palace Hotel Grill, though there were those who insisted that Manning's Restaurant had really created the style long before, calling it "Oysters Salt Roast." For that matter, the Palace Hotel Grill had long been good enough to draw praise from such distinguished visitors as General U. S. Grant, Jay Gould, and Chester A. Arthur. By the nineties it was established in its unique position; its chefs had made their specialties famous around the world, featuring mountain quail, abalone, and the California Oyster Omelet. So well known was the Grill's excellence, in fact, that when it was redecorated in the late nineties the reporters who attended the grand reopening found themselves out of adjectives, one of them solving the problem by falling back on the French tag that was on everyone's lips then, and writing simply, "The Palace Grill is the *fin de siècle* in café cuisine in America. It has no peer."

The significant thing about San Francisco's gastronomic history, however, is that good food was not merely the privilege of the well-to-do.

Once established, the habit of "eating out" remained and remains to this day a San Francisco custom. And although the more luxurious restaurants could boast that they were known to all the gourmets of the world, the city developed and supported dozens of smaller places where those who knew could find food unsurpassed by any of the great chefs. Up to the earthquake and fire of 1906, Bazzuro's Restaurant on lower Pacific Street provided the finest pastes, risottos, and scallopini for those who liked Italian dishes. So did Perini's on Post Street. For that matter, San Francisco's large Italian colony still can show the visitor a trick or two; no one who has picked the pearly meat from a cracked crab cooked in the enormous kettles on Fisherman's Wharf will ever forget its sweetness. The French and the Germans added their bit; you may find men today who will tell you with tears in their eyes about the sauerbraten and potato pancakes at the old Hofbrau or the Heidelberg Inn, and the salad dressing for which Blanco's was once famous. Older men can go back to the days of the Mint Restaurant in Commercial Street and Billy Jackson's southern fried chicken. Younger ones will rhapsodize over broiled sea bass in butter at Big John's. Such connoisseurs will talk to you for hours if you but mention Johnson's Oyster House or Marshall's Chop House, or Martin's which was made famous by the "Comstock crowd." In the second decade of this century, Bigin's, which prohibition pried loose from Columbus Avenue and finally killed, vied with Coppa's for the patronage of the younger writers and artists, though Coppa's great dish, Chicken Portola, gave him a precious advantage. Though this is a cookbook in which the author proposes to introduce to you the delicacies of Armenian cuisine, perhaps it will do no harm to reproduce here Coppa's own recipe for that delectable dish as old Clarence Edwords quoted it in his naïvely written little gastronomes' treasure, *Bohemian San Francisco*. Here is Chicken Portola, à la Coppa:

Take a fresh cocoanut and cut off the top, removing nearly all of the meat. Put together 3 tablespoonfuls of chopped cocoanut meat and 2 ears of fresh green corn taken from the cob. Slice 2 onions into 4 tablespoonfuls of the best olive oil, together with a tablespoonful of diced bacon fried in olive oil, add 1 chopped green pepper, half a dozen tomatoes stewed with salt and pepper, 1 clove of garlic, and cook all together until it thickens. Strain this into the corn and cocoanut and add 1 spring chicken cut in 4 pieces. Put the mixture into the shell of the cocoanut, using the cut-off top as a cover, and close tightly with a covering of flour-and-water paste around the jointure to keep in the flavors. Put the cocoanut into a pan of water and set in a hot oven for 1 hour, basting frequently to prevent the cocoanut's burning.

But even to list the restaurants of the early 1900s would require pages of print. Wallace Irwin meant what he said when he wrote, "Half the town was restaurants, and all of them were good!" The point is that the San Franciscan's palate was educated by them, encouraged by the variety of their food and drink to know good cooking and to go where it could be obtained. And though it is human to regret the passing of the old and to be skeptical of the new, the honest gourmet will tell you that San Francisco today has dozens of restaurants in which the city's traditions in food and drink survive and flourish. Perhaps Camille's is gone, but Pierre's is still there. Jack's will still do you a Rex Sole in chopped herbs and white wine that is worth crossing the city to eat. The Odeon became a cafeteria in the twenties, but Fred Solari in Maiden Lane has not forgotten how to be lavish with his oil and sparing with his wine vinegar when he mixes you a green salad with crab-legs. In Chinatown there are half a dozen places in any of which you may get an incomparably fine Chinese dinner with no hint, even, of the fearsome "chop suey" that sells to the tourist trade. Over on the fringes of North Beach are Spanish and Mexican restaurants where the *chiles rellenos* will make your mouth water and not scorch your throat, either. You may eat in San Francisco in the Basque manner if you like, or find a little Athenian café where you can get the small Greek olives and the goat's milk *feta* which burns the tongue, maybe a tiny glass of *ouzo,* and of course the thick, sweet Turkish coffee that you can drink, cup after syrupy cup, and come back for more. Yes, you can eat in San Francisco today as well as ever.

But with the coffee we come full cycle, and back to George Mardikian and Omar Khayyam's, whose coffee, although it is made in the Turkish manner, it is better to call by some other name since, from his Armenian boyhood, George remembers Turks with no particular pleasure.

Omar Khayyam's is an Armenian restaurant with a Persian name in an American city. George had a good reason for selecting that name. It is the legend that Omar, the Persian tentmaker, might have been content to stitch his lengths of cloth all his days if an Armenian had not introduced him to the delights of the wine-cup he was to celebrate so notably. Omar's pious Mohammedan abstention, if the story is true, dissolved before the sad-eyed logic of his Armenian friend, and the two of them got royally drunk together. It was then that, for the first time in his life, Omar's lips uttered, of all things, poetry. And George Mardikian regards the whole thing as the simplest, most obvious chain of circumstances. Since it was an Armenian who first brought wine and Omar together, thus producing the *Rubaiyat,* what more sensible than to call an Armenian restaurant by the name of the great Persian? To be sure, Omar's is a name Americans know, too. Mardikian possesses, above all things, good common sense in a business way.

As far as George himself is concerned, William Saroyan introduces him to you in the Foreword, and George will tell you quite simply about his life in the first chapter of his book, and about how he came to be interested in food, in cookery, and eventually in the history of eating which he has studied over half the civilized world. He will even try to tell you that there was somewhere, back in the dim past, some connection between the Armenians and the Scots; in Armenia, he argues, they play bagpipes, and there is an Armenian dish which is enough like a Scots haggis to deceive the real McKay. And the surname Haig is one of Armenia's oldest.

These things you may believe or not as you choose. What George really wants in this book is to tell you something about how he cooks the food that has won his Omar Khayyam's in San Francisco a secure place in a city famous from its beginnings for providing gustatory pleasures. What he wants, too, is to show the American woman how she may prepare these dishes in her own kitchen, and without searching for rare or exotic ingredients. It is George's belief that one of the great results of World War II has been the fact that it forced the American woman to forget the can opener and think about what to do with the simplest foods. So thinking, she may learn new things; indeed, she cannot help learning them if she reads this book.

George Mardikian, you see, is a man who thinks a great deal about happiness, perhaps because he had so little of it in his childhood, in a country where every ten-year-old carried a rock in his pocket against the Turk. He believes, with Brillat-Savarin, that "the discovery of a new dish does more for the happiness of mankind than the discovery of a star." Wherefore here is your opportunity to make such discoveries for yourself, all the way from Derevapatat, which is simply stuffed grape leaves, to Ekmek Khadiyaff with Kaymak, which is a dessert that a great Armenian chef, Tocatlian, created for the Empress Eugénie, and which, as George makes it—and as you can make it if you will consult pages 141 and 142 of this work—has drawn

superlatives from personalities as diverse as the late O. O. Mc-
Intyre, Rudy Vallee, Eleanor Roosevelt, and Orson Welles. In
fact, if there is in you the faintest trace of what Louis Unter-
meyer called "the rapture and response of food," you will already be impatient to get into the text.

San Francisco,
California.
May 1944.

Here's How, America

WAR has injected into the American kitchen unfamiliar restrictions—rationing and scarcities. But as it is hoped the recipes in this book will continue to serve their useful purpose long after the war, no substitutions have been indicated. When necessary, however, substitutes such as margarine for butter, honey for sugar, and milk for cream may be used.

No rare and expensive ingredients are indicated in any of the recipes; many of the recipes do not require foods that have a high point value, and most materials are easily obtainable. For those fortunate enough to have a victory garden, vegetables that are commonly home grown are included in the stews and other dishes.

Out of the challenge to the ingenuity of the American housewife that rationing presents should grow a new American cuisine, combining the best of the cooking of other nationalities. It will be developed, not by chefs, but by housewives who will grow to love their own kitchens and prefer their own creations to the tin can and can opener.

There are many cookbooks, new and old, but mine, I hope, will not be just an ordinary cookbook, for I am dedicating it to America and Americans. The thing that has prompted me to do so is the extreme gratefulness I feel for this country and what it has done for me and my people.

This book is intended to introduce the type of cuisine that Armenians have lived on for centuries, in spite of scarcity and deprivation. Unfortunately, the cuisine of the Near East has

15

not been properly presented to America. It has been confined mainly to small national groups catering to their own people and representing mostly the working class. But many people who want to make a party of dining out hesitate to go to a place like this unless they feel like "slumming." This is true of most foreign foods. People who want a real Chinese dinner will not go to a much-publicized Chinese restaurant, because there the Chinese dishes will have become Americanized.

My aim here is to give authentic Armenian dishes, prepared in the Armenian manner, but seasoned for the American palate.

Recipes in this book represent some of the choice and accepted dishes of world-famous personalities—movie, radio, and stage stars, literary figures and royalty—and many that have been devised for good, plain, food-loving Americans. These recipes, also, represent twenty years of research and experimentation in practically every corner of the earth.

I have not been particular what jobs I have had to take in famous hotels and restaurants in order to learn the secrets of chefs noted the world over. For instance, I remember getting a job in Alexandria, Egypt, so that I could work near the famous restaurateur, Ashji Mugurdich, who was a great chef in the palaces of the sultans and pashas in Constantinople (now called Istanbul). He also worked as chef of the Tocatlian Hotel, the most popular place to eat in Constantinople.

Here I worked from sunup to sundown. My wages were five dollars a week. Somehow this old fox found out that I was living at a French *pension,* and he knew that rentals there were never less than six dollars. So it worried him.

One morning I came to work and as I walked in I said "Good morning." Usually he would answer cordially. But this morning he said nothing. I thought probably he had had a bad night, or a fight with his wife, or something, so I left him alone.

During the course of our work I would ask for certain things.

No answer. This went on for a couple of hours, until finally I got tired of the whole thing. I said, "What is eating you? Why don't you answer me?"

Slowly he laid down his knife, and walked toward me. "Where do you live?"

"Why?" I asked.

"I want to know. Where do you live?"

"At the French *pension*."

"How much do you pay?"

"Six dollars a week."

"That doesn't make sense, does it?"

"I don't know what you are driving at," I told him.

"Well," he said, "how can a man who is making five dollars a week pay six dollars for room rent?"

Naturally I didn't want to explain that the only reason I was working for him was to try to learn his cooking secrets. So I said, "Well, it is not my fault that you don't pay your help enough."

That didn't convince him, but he shook his head and went back to work. Two or three minutes later he came over to me again. In a whispering voice he said, "Tell me, did you murder someone in the United States?"

He had put two and two together and figured that here was a man who must have killed someone, stolen his money, and was hiding from the police. Now no one in America would ever think of a thing like that. One must have a very suspicious, Near Eastern mind to come to such a conclusion.

Fortunately, I had already arranged for my passage to Naples, so I decided to tell him, "I quit. The reason I was working for you was to learn your culinary secrets for my patrons in my beloved America."

Somehow this explanation touched him very much. Whereas before that every time he mixed a new dish he would turn his back to me, now he couldn't do enough for me. He tried to teach me everything he knew. We had a very fine dinner together the night before I left, and he promised to send me his favorite recipes as he thought of them. He kept his promise, and corresponded with me for years. Unfortunately, his handwriting was very bad, and I could not make it out. So if I am not able to duplicate some of his wonderful delicacies, put it down to that fact.

On another occasion I was able to secure some of my most prized recipes from the Armenian Monastery on Saint Lazarus Island. This one is called Mekhetarian Vank, and it was here Lord Byron studied Armenian. I consider myself honored to be able to pass along some of the things that I learned from the great scholar there, the Right Reverend Hatzouni.

This monastery was the printing shop for the Venetian government. In this institution you find one of the greatest collections of old manuscripts. Some of them weigh hundreds of pounds, and require two or three monks to lift them. They have the same beautiful and artistic colorings as Armenian and Oriental rugs, and the ages have not dimmed them. It was through those musty old manuscripts that I came to realize that Armenian cuisine goes back 3900 years. Here also I found accounts for the first time of a beverage called beer, which was drunk from mugs through long straws.

In these same manuscripts I discovered the first gourmet of Armenia. He was King Shara, who moved his capital from one section of the country to another because he found better barley and fruits there. Later I give the recipe for his famous Royal Soup. The capital that he built was called Shirag, and is the present Aleksandropol or Leninakan. In the remote sections of Armenia, especially high in the Caucasian mountains, where the natives have had few dealings with city folks, you still find the customs and proverbs originated by King Shara.

For instance, I remember traveling through the Kharakelesa.

There being no hotels or inns, I was guest of the mayor of the city, who was also the chief of police, fireman, judge, and everything else combined. The old grandmother, who in this region is head of the family, after watching me eat more than my share, called my attention to this proverb: "My son, if your appetite is King Shara's appetite, please remember that our warehouses are not as full as his." In other words, "Go easy."

I believe a man must be born a great chef. He must be born an artist as surely as Rembrandt, and he must carry with him a genius for creating fine food. This gift, if I have it, I assure you comes from my beloved mother who, through her excellent preparations for our family, gave me my first appreciation of fine foods.

I know everyone thinks his or her mother's cooking is the best in the world. I have tried to analyze why this should be, and after having suffered through many "wonderful dinners" cooked by mothers, I have come to the conclusion that mother's cooking tastes best to the person who has grown up with that cooking. They crave that particular type of cuisine. It is common knowledge that some of our wealthiest men, who can afford to dine in the finest restaurants, look forward to the day when they can visit some remote village to partake of mother's cooking—which in some cases, I must say, is very bad.

Since I am supposed to know something about food, I may say that *my* mother does not fall into the latter category. I think it is because of her that I have been able to please patrons and gourmets from every corner of the earth. And this is an everlasting debt I owe to my mother.

I remember when I was able to bring her over to this country. We had delayed the grand opening of the now famous Omar Khayyam's in the city of Fresno until the day of her arrival. Over 530 guests were present. We had direct radio hook-up

The mayor and many city and county officials were there, and the affair was a grand success.

Fresnans were so free with their praises and testimonials that I, who can never stop talking, was speechless. All I could do was shed tears of joy. Of course my eyes were focused on the table where my mother was sitting with my wife and sister. I could see that her big blue eyes were also brimming with tears— tears of happiness that her son was a success in America, that he had accomplished something in this wonderful land, and she was witnessing it.

As the party ended many of my friends, among them newspaper and radio people and home economists, rushed over and started demanding recipes for the dishes on that night's menu. Naturally we spoke in English and my mother couldn't understand a word of it. Finally she asked me what all these people wanted. I told her they were cooking experts, and they wanted my recipes. She was practically bursting with pride that her son could give to Americans something they wanted. I mean that she felt that I, as a representative of the Armenian people who are so grateful to America, could help in this small way to pay back part of our debt.

My sister Baidzar, who was sitting at the same table, had been in America longer than I. She turned to me, and speaking in Armenian, warned me not to give my recipes away. They were my stock in trade. But at that point my mother interrupted.

"My darling daughter," she said, "do you not remember our neighbor Makrouhi Hanum? For forty years I have taught her how to cook *plaki,* and she still can't make it as I can." She turned to me and in a confident voice said, "Son, give them all the recipes they ask for. They could never cook them as you do anyway."

I am of the same opinion as my mother. It was her pride speaking, of course, but it is true that there are hardly any two people who cook alike. Anyone who likes to cook can always better a recipe that has been passed on to him.

Realizing all of this, I have selected from a vast collection of recipes for our readers dishes that are not only exotic and different but are beneficial to health and simple to prepare. There are no recipes here for which the ingredients are difficult to find.

Recipes presented here depend largely on the innate goodness of the food itself and its flavors, and on preparing and seasoning it as simply as possible. There are no complicated blendings of seasoning or ingredients designed to disguise bad meat or bad cooking. My idea of a good cook is not one who boils the flavor out of meat and then pours a dubious sauce over it at the serving table. A truly good cook prepares and cooks food so as to preserve its goodness and flavor. Drugstore condiments will then be unnecessary to render the food palatable. Roasting and baking foods is the secret for sealing in the natural flavors, especially in the Armenian cuisine. Thus by cooking foods in the manner explained in the following chapters, the reader will discover that "natural flavors sealed in" also means that the nourishing vitamins and health-giving values of the foods are also preserved. It is all in the method of cooking. So let us not boil away vitamins, or cover up flavors with the lavish use of condiments.

Another and very important point is to make eating a ceremony instead of just a matter of habit. There is no better time to enjoy the company of one's family and friends than during a well-planned meal. Also (and husbands please take note) a little appreciation goes a long way toward making a good cook. A well-chosen compliment will help greatly toward improving the quality of your wife's cooking and spur her on to greater effort. This is the secret of the fame of all chefs. They must continue to improve to live up to their reputations. And, by way of advice to wives: Serve your husband the things you yourself enjoy, because you will then see that these foods are prepared to the n-n-nnth degree.

I discovered some years ago that one of the reasons Americans do things so well is because they enjoy doing them. They enjoy life. It was difficult for me to learn this, for Armenians are innately a melancholy people, a people subjected to many wars, massacres, and hardships.

When I first came to America as a young man of twenty-two, fresh from the horrible wars in the Near East, from murder and torture, I knew what it meant at first hand to be starved and frozen and left for dead in the snows of winter. And when I escaped these tortures and came to America, it was like coming to Heaven. As a child I remember my first glimpse of Mt. Ararat, which is the most majestic sight to every Armenian. Across a hot valley and far up into the sky this snow-covered mountain rises nearly 17,000 feet, with two peaks. This mountain was the legendary resting place for Noah's Ark. I shall never forget it. But there are also bitter memories of Armenia, and I shall never forget the new thrill I had when, as an immigrant boy, I saw the Statue of Liberty as we came into New York Harbor. Here was relief from torture and heartbreak, and I felt it with all my heart. At that moment, I decided to leave all hatred and bitterness behind and begin life anew; like the many wonderful things we had heard about America in Armenia, the Statue of Liberty seemed to symbolize them all that day.

When we arrived at Ellis Island, immigration officers inspected us, gave us a shower and changed our clothes. That shower seemed to wash all the ugliness of the world away forever. My brother Arshag had wired from San Francisco to tell us he had my railroad tickets, and so I set out to cross the United States. Since I could not speak a word of English or understand anything that was said to me, my ticket was pinned to the lapel of my coat; this had my name and destination on it. People were kind and smiled at me; the contrast was so great, it was hard to believe that people could be as happy and cheerful as I saw them that day on the train. Everything I saw inspired me with an ambition to be one of them. I thought of many things, and decided I should go to school immediately, study English and learn how to be a good American.

The cross-country trip was not without momentary excitement and misgivings. Coming into Kansas City, the Traveler's Aid Society took charge of me. During the stopover I looked out into a street and saw thousands of men wearing fezzes marching toward the depot. My God, I thought, are there Turks over here too? And I reached instinctively into my pocket for the rock I invariably carried at home as protection against them. When they came closer, I realized they were not dressed quite right and they seemed too happy to be Turks. I believe the first thing I asked my sister when I reached San Francisco was who these people were. She told me they were Shriners who had been to a convention.

The following day was Sunday. My family took me on a tour of San Francisco, and we went to the beach. It was a bright clear day and it was a marvelous sight to see thousands of people playing in the sand, laughing and having a hilarious time. Women and children were swimming and riding the Chutes, and even old men with whiskers were throwing balls and playing leapfrog. I couldn't understand it.

Are these people crazy? I asked myself. In our country when people grow up they are solemn and have dignity. For years I had not seen them laugh and play. What is the matter with these people? I thought.

This bothered me. That night I couldn't eat or sleep thinking about my first day here. I remember my sister and brother talking about me and wondering what was wrong. The next morning I decided to see the city by myself and walked many blocks until I was exhausted. However, I remained on the same street so I wouldn't get lost. What I saw was amazing. I saw men with pails going to work. They were whistling. Milkmen were humming quietly as they left bottles on the doorsteps. The motorman on the cable car was whistling merrily as he pulled on the brakes. Even the street-sweeper smiled at me as he cheerily called, "Good morning." He didn't even know me. But I smiled back.

Suddenly I had it! I rushed home to my sister, and ran into the kitchen yelling, "These Americans are not crazy. They are right. We are wrong. It is right to be happy. You feel better. You make the other fellow feel better. I am going to be a happy American; no more thinking sad thoughts, making sad music, and dwelling on the woes of our people."

Since then, my ability to smile has been of the greatest help. I could smile when I couldn't talk English, and while I was learning to cook. I think my ability to smile, even when I was losing money, gained me the many friends who have made the restaurants a success. That, and the fact that I believe if you have something worth while people will go far to get it. Like the old story about the mousetrap—well, that theory holds good in the restaurant business, too. If the food is good enough, people will come to the restaurant even if it is in the middle of the desert.

As to cooking, I think few people have burned their fingers as often as I have. I was always lifting up the cover of the pot to see what my mother was cooking, trying to steal a piece of delicious-smelling meat. I guess my cooking experience dates back to long before I was ten years old, because I always liked to go to the shores of the Bosporus in Constantinople, where I would find mussels, make a fire, and throw them in. We cooked shrimps and all kinds of fish that way. Sometimes we weren't so successful. I remember one day we tried to cook a turtle. We had the hardest time breaking that turtle. We finally broke the under shell with rocks; then we tried to broil the meat. If you have ever tried this method of cooking turtle, you will know that we couldn't even chew it. We finally borrowed a pot and boiled it for six hours, but it just got tougher and tougher. You can see that I learned cooking the hard way.

I was called Shishko (Chubby) when I was a little boy, because I loved to eat. I think, looking back on it, that the most pleasant moments of my childhood were the times when my father took us to the *locanta,* or restaurants, and we could order any of the delicacies that we couldn't get at home.

In Constantinople every bar used to have a stand right in front of it where for five cents one could get fried liver with onions and parsley. On many occasions, after a big dinner at home, I would sneak down to this forbidden corner by myself and buy my five cents' worth of liver *piaz.* I would always get caught because my mother would get a whiff of the onions—or maybe it was because of my guilty look.

One of my earliest cooking experiences was when we first organized the Boy Scout movement in Constantinople. We had an Athletic Club which changed its name to the Boy Scouts. It was under the supervision and leadership of Muguer Muguerian, who had lived in America. We would go to camp for three months of our vacation. I was always hanging around the cook, and long before the three months were up, I would be doing all of the cooking for the camp.

Later, when I was with the Armenian Legion during the First World War, food was our most acute problem. Because we Armenians were sort of stepsons to the Russian army, if there wasn't enough food to go around, we didn't eat. The only time we had a decent meal was when we captured a town. I would find a lamb, kill it, make a fire and roast it. But we couldn't wait until it was properly roasted. As soon as it was hot through, we ate it. There was no lighting system there, of course, so we would do all this by firelight. Many a time in the morning I would look at the carved carcass of the lamb, and wonder how we had eaten all that raw meat!

But that was many years ago, and a far cry from this land of plenty in which we live and breathe the air of freedom, and where we have such an abundance and variety of food to work with. So now let's get on with our recipes and our cooking.

Madzoon

I CONSIDER that an outstanding contribution to my adopted land is my effort to encourage Americans to eat madzoon.

Madzoon is a great energy builder. People in the restaurant business put in ungodly long hours. Take my case, for example. All day I have to be on the job to see that everything goes right. Added to this are my other varied activities such as speaking engagements, radio work, welfare work, in addition to my restaurants in Fresno and San Francisco, not to mention two sandwich shops! It is enough to keep anybody hopping twenty-four hours a day. At ten o'clock at night I am physically and mentally very tired. Then I sit down at a table in my restaurant, and without ordering, the waiter will set before me a bowl of madzoon. When I finish eating it, I feel as though I had just come to work. Truly!

But don't take my word alone for it. The great scientist, Dr. Élie Metchnikoff, attributes the stamina and longevity of all the Balkan peoples to nothing so much as this food. They and people from the Caucasus are practically immune to stomach ailments and ulcers. Yet they are among the poorest peoples in the world, and are deprived of many vitamin-giving foods. They give credit for their good health to madzoon.

Madzoon is the same as yoghurt, as it is known in all Balkan countries, and as laban in Arabic countries such as Syria, Iran, Egypt, and North Africa. It is also the same as koumis, which has been used for centuries in the Mongol countries. In fact, Genghis Khan actually lived on it during those long marches through Mongolia when other food was hard to obtain.

Madzoon has beneficial bacteria that work like yeast. And it is very simple to prepare. You take a little madzoon and put it into milk. The bacteria, when mixed with milk, begin to grow and multiply. The more they multiply, the more sour the milk becomes. When we speak of the "starter" for madzoon, we mean either the bacteria that are produced in this way or the madzoon itself. To obtain this starter, just open any telephone book and find a name ending with "ian." Go to that person's address, knock on the door, and ask the Armenian who opens it for a cup of madzoon. If he doesn't have it, he will certainly tell you where to get it. Then you are all set for life, for the madzoon keeps on growing like yeast, and you make the new batch with a starter from the last.

To prepare madzoon, boil a quart of milk to a point where it is ready to go over the top of the pan. Then let it cool off until it is lukewarm, or so that there will be a little sting when you test a drop of it on your wrist. Then put a tablespoonful of madzoon from a former batch in a cup and dissolve it in some of the warm milk. When thoroughly dissolved, pour it into the quart of warm milk. Mix well, then pour into individual cups to set. Use crockery, glass, or earthen cups which will retain the heat. Do not use metal.

Now cover the cups with a breadboard, then cover with a heavy towel to retain the warmth, and keep in a warm place. In 8 hours the madzoon will be ready. It will have reached the consistency of custard. Remove cover and store in the refrigerator. This madzoon will keep for about 3 days, but I suggest making it every other day, for it becomes too strong to suit the taste of most palates.

A person should eat a pint of madzoon a day. A quart of milk makes 5 or 6 cups, depending on their size.

Appetizers and Cocktails

APPETIZERS in Armenia are most often composed of pickled fresh vegetables and fruits. They differ from the ordinary pickles we find in our markets in that, instead of pickling them with vinegar, the Armenians use the centuries-old barley and wheat process of fermentation. This method is used generally in the Nordic countries and in Russia, where they preserve large quantities of sauerkraut and kapousta.

Although eating raw vegetables has become a fad in America because of newly discovered food values, it has long been a custom in Armenia. Vegetables such as carrots, cucumbers, and the hearts of cabbage are eaten like fruit. When I was a child, we ate them as American youngsters eat raw apples. Whenever we had cabbage for dinner, we would hang around Mother until she would cut out the core of the cabbage and give it to us. We ate raw peppers, too, which we call too-too peppers when they are pickled.

MIXED VEGETABLE PICKLES

Armennettes

Select fresh round carrots, celery, green tomatoes, long banana-like eggplant, peppers, cabbage, and cauliflower. Peel carrots, and cut all vegetables into convenient size for serving. Mix all together.

Now put a handful of barley in a barrel or large earthenware jug. Add a handful of whole mixed spices. If you like the flavor of garlic, cut up a few cloves, tie them in a cheesecloth bag and hang inside the jar so that it can be taken out and thrown away when the flavor is strong enough.

Then start putting in the vegetables. After 3 or 4 inches high, sprinkle generously with salt. Continue this process until the jar is filled. If you like your pickles hot, and your whole spice does not include chilis, buy some small Spanish green peppers and place them throughout the mixture.

When you come to the top layer, cover with water. Lay a round piece of wood or a plate on top and put a weight on it to press it down. Let the jar stand for a week in a cold place, then mix up the vegetables and cover again in the same manner. It will take about 3 weeks to completely pickle the vegetables, the time depending upon the temperature.

If you are in a hurry for your pickles, you can make practically the same thing in 5 days by using vinegar instead of barley. For this method, boil together 1 pint of vinegar, 1 tablespoonful of allspice, 3 tablespoonfuls of salt, and pour this over the fresh vegetables. When the hot vinegar touches the vegetables, it softens them, and they absorb the vinegar and spices rapidly. Pour water to cover the mixture, and let stand for 5 days as in the above method. The barley method of pickling is supposed to make vegetables more digestible than the vinegar method.

GREGORIAN COCKTAIL
Mixed Vegetable Cocktail

This cocktail is named after the Armenian Gregorian Christian Church. It is so called especially because it is eaten during the meatless lenten season which lasts for 40 days. In the interior of Armenia this dish, and bread, are the only things the people eat during this time, for they are very careful how they observe Lent. The cocktail is a really palatable and delicious food.

2 cupfuls catsup

¼ cup pickled relish

1 cupful of broiled and mixed chopped green peppers,
   onions, and tomatoes

6 dashes tabasco sauce

1 teaspoonful Worcestershire sauce

1/6 teaspoonful white or black pepper

1½ teaspoonfuls salt

½ teaspoonful finely chopped fresh or dry mint

½ cup juice of pickled grape leaves

Broil vegetables (I really mean *broil,* either over charcoal
or on the gas broiler), and chop very fine. Mix all ingredients
and chill. Keep in refrigerator. When serving, cover top with
chopped walnuts.

DEREVAPATAT or DOLMA
Stuffed Grape Leaves

There are many ways to prepare dolmas. *Dolma* means
"stuffed." Favorite of the Armenians, and of most of my patrons in America, is stuffed grape leaves. These are used as an
appetizer and are served cold. Cabbage may be stuffed, rolled,
and cooked, and served cold; also squash, tomatoes, and eggplant. But the most tempting of all is the real dolma of grape
leaves.

According to Armenian legend, this dish dates back to the
time of Noah's Ark. It is the belief of Armenians that when
the floods subsided, Noah got off the ark and settled in Nakhichevan. This word means "first stop." Incidentally, the town
still exists with the same name and, strange as it seems, it hasn't
changed much in appearance since Biblical times. The people
live practically the same way they did then.

It is said that lack of vegetation following the flood compelled Noah and his family to eat grape leaves. They had been on the Ark all that time with no green vegetables. Many will ask, "But why grape leaves?"

Anyone who lives in valleys where there are vineyards knows that after either a drought or flood season, the first plant to sprout leaves will be the grapevine. This is true in the Nakhichevan section which has the distinction of having the oldest vineyards in the world. If anyone is inclined to quarrel with my theory, let me point out the passage in the Bible from Genesis where it is recorded that Noah, a husbandman, made wine and got drunk. So he must have had grapes. Hence my conclusion that grape leaves were eaten for the first time in Armenia. But let's see how we make dolma.

    2 cups peanut or olive oil
    5 cups onions, chopped
    1 cup uncooked rice
    1 cup parsley chopped fine
    ½ cup currants or seedless raisins
    ½ cup pine nuts (optional)
    ½ cup tomato sauce or purée
    1 cup water
    ½ teaspoonful allspice
    ½ teaspoonful cinnamon
    2 tablespoonfuls salt
    ½ teaspoonful black pepper
    grape leaves

Pour oil into cooking pot. Add onions and sauté until golden brown. Add rice and cook, covered, for ½ hour with the onions.

Then add all other ingredients and cook for 5 minutes. Let cool a little. Then put a teaspoonful of this mixture on each grape leaf and roll it up like a package. In the bottom of a baking pan place some sliced onions, lettuce, or grape leaves. This will prevent dolmas from burning. Put stuffed, rolled leaves side by side in pan. Put a large plate over them, and pour water over to cover plate. Cook on a slow fire for 1 hour. Let them cool in the pot, then put in refrigerator to chill. Serve as an appetizer, salad, or cold entree. I have purposely given the amount of ingredients for a large portion because you may keep them on hand in the refrigerator all the time. These dolmas are delicious and different.

SHRIMP AND CRAB LEGS IN CABBAGE

One of the most attractive ways to eat shrimp or crab is in cocktails, as they are served around the Black Sea. Hollow out a cabbage, then fill it with a sauce similar to Thousand Island dressing. Stick colored toothpicks into the outside of the cabbage, and surround it with shrimps and crab legs. Everyone takes a toothpick, spears a piece of crab meat or shrimp, and dunks it in the dressing.

Fun, and very pretty for cocktail parties!

ARTICHOKES

Artichokes are a product of the Mediterranean country and all around Asia Minor. They are used there more than any place I've been. And I think the Levantines are true artists in creating artichoke dishes. I have found that only chefs or cooks in Constantinople know how to do justice to this vegetable. They have become such masters that they know all the temperament of the artichoke. When you take off the outside leaves, for instance, the leaves immediately get black. To prevent this, rub them with the inside of used lemon rinds, thereby, incidentally, making the most of the lemons. Then, to improve the flavor, boil the artichoke with a very small onion.

ARTICHOKES BYZANTINE

6 large artichokes
2 medium-sized onions, sliced
1 tablespoonful sugar
juice of 2 lemons
⅔ cupful olive or peanut oil
1 cupful water
salt and pepper

Cut artichoke leaves in half crosswise and save bottoms. Put bottoms in cooking pot; add lemon juice, sliced onions, sugar, oil, seasonings, and water. Cover tightly and cook for 1 hour on a medium fire. *Do not open cover while cooking.* Serve cold as appetizer or salad, with juice and onions poured over artichoke heart. This may also be served hot as a vegetable.

DABGODZ SEMPOOG
Fried Eggplant

To my amazement, when I first arrived in the United States I found that Americans knew very little about eggplant. The only way eggplant was served in restaurants or homes was the ordinary way of dipping it into batter and frying it. Most of the time it was not even appetizing.

At my restaurant we serve it at least 120 different ways. I dare anyone to call me on that, because he will then be compelled to dine for 120 days at my place, and I will give him a different eggplant dish every day. There are probably hundreds of other ways to prepare it with which I am not familiar, but up to now I have had no difficulty in popularizing our eggplant specialties, which have become unusual delicacies. Dabgodz Sempoog is the type of appetizer that can be prepared in a short time and it can be preserved in the refrigerator for quite a few days. Now if you want to fry eggplant, try this method.

2 large peeled, sliced eggplants
1 cup oil
2 cloves of garlic
½ cup of vinegar
salt

Peel and slice eggplant. Salt well, and let it stand for ½ hour. Heat oil in frying pan, add chopped garlic, and sauté. Wash salted, sliced eggplant and dry on a towel. Then fry in oil to a golden brown color. Take out and set in deep dish. Pour vinegar over while hot, and let stand for 15 minutes. Drain off vinegar. Chill eggplant and serve as an appetizer or side vegetable dish.

As you will notice in the directions, I say salt the eggplant well. The purpose of this is to take the bitterness out. You can actually see the eggplant perspire.

DABGODZ TETOOM
Fried Squash

This appetizer is cooked and prepared in the same way as the eggplant dish, only zucchini is used instead. Zucchini is cut lengthwise into ⅓-inch-thick slices. Do not peel.

MELONIZED PINEAPPLE

Take a good-sized fresh pineapple, and cut it lengthwise into 4 sections. Leave the green stem on it, and be sure to cut it so that some of the leaves stay with each section of pineapple. Cut out the core. Slice through the pineapple meat down to the rind. Pour over each section grenadine or maraschino cherry juice. Serve very cold, and you have a beautiful appetizer.

CALIFORNIA SUMMER COCKTAIL

Use plenty of oranges, and plenty of melons, preferably three kinds: casaba, Persian, and watermelon. Scoop out melon with a ball spoon. Drop the balls into plain sugar syrup, then add cubed orange sections and sliced bananas. Chill and serve in a bowl. To add a tang to it, add a cupful of boiled, chilled raisins, and pour over the fruit a little California sherry or muscatel wine.

TOPIG
Garbanzo Appetizer

Soak 1 pound of garbanzos, or chick peas, overnight and boil them until tender. Then grind them up with a boiled potato. Make a round layer of the resulting paste. Shape it like a bowl and stuff it with the following mixture:

Sauté 1 cupful chopped onions in 3 tablespoonfuls of olive or peanut oil. Add 2 tablespoonfuls of chopped parsley and pine nuts. Flavor with tahin, which is the essence of sesame seeds. Stuff this mixture into the paste cake, wrap in cheesecloth, and mold into any shape you like (we usually make it like a salami). Boil in salted water for at least 1 hour. Let it get cold in the cheesecloth. It forms a crust when cool. Remove cheesecloth, slice and serve as an hors d'oeuvre.

Soups

THE finest and most respected recipe that has come out of the Caucasus is the one for Arkayagan Abour or Royal Soup. It is also known as Victory Soup. This dish is served in Armenia only on very special occasions, like the birth of a baby boy, or the return of the oldest son from a pilgrimage that has perhaps taken as long as twenty years, for the boy may have gone to a foreign country to earn money and then come home to settle down. This is the perfect time to serve Royal Soup. It is also prepared when townspeople are honoring a distinguished national leader or foreign visitor.

I have found records of the authentic origin of Royal Soup in monasteries located in various parts of old Armenia. Here Armenian monks have saved the most precious Armenian manuscripts for sixteen centuries. It was in one of these fifteen-hundred-year-old manuscripts that I found out why this soup is called Royal or Victory Soup. Over thirty-five hundred years ago, when an Armenian king went to war and came back victorious it was his solemn duty to go into the rich forests and bring back all sorts of wild birds and gazelles. He would bring the game to the palace steps where a huge *gatsa,* or kettle, had been placed by coppersmiths. After his servants had cleaned the gazelles and birds, the king with his own hands would prepare the Royal Soup and serve it to the princes and princesses of his court, who in turn would serve the public who had come from every part of Armenia to celebrate the victory.

As the years went by and game and birds became scarce,

Armenians tried to find other ways to make the soup. Now, instead of serving huge chunks of gazelle and pheasant meat, they substitute chicken broth, and make the meat balls out of deer meat. As culinary art has progressed, they have added zest to the soup. In the olden days they used to put young grapes into the soup for flavoring. Now they add lemon juice and eggs beaten together. It gives a delightful flavor that you can't find in anything else.

Not having any gazelles available in America, I have substituted venison in my recipes. One of the most important dinners I have served in America was when A. E. Nelson, then vice-president and general manager of NBC in San Francisco, commissioned me to serve the most perfect meal I could prepare to the visiting NBC president, Niles Trammell. Fortunately, just before the dinner, the deer season opened, so I sent off two of my boys, who were good hunters, to get me a buck. I knew they wouldn't come back empty-handed. We had a 135-pound buck from which we prepared the Royal Soup à la Niles Trammell.

ARKAYAGAN ABOUR
Royal Soup

½ gallon chicken broth
½ pound venison meat, ground
½ cupful bulghour, finely ground wheat, or rice
¼ cupful very finely chopped onion
¼ cupful very finely chopped parsley
juice of 2 lemons
3 eggs (raw)
salt and pepper

Mix raw meat, rice, onions, parsley, and seasonings together. Make mixture into small balls about the size of hazelnuts. Drop into the chicken broth and cook for about 1 hour. Mix the juice of the 2 lemons with the raw eggs and beat well. Then slowly pour the soup broth into the egg and lemon mixture, beating constantly, until all the broth has been used. Pour over the meat balls and serve immediately.

DARON ABOUR
Barley Soup

Daron is the place, and *abour* means soup. This soup is named after a section in Armenia which has produced not only the finest fighters and warriors but has also given to Armenia its greatest literary figures of the past. It was Mesrob Mashdotz and Sahag Gatoghigos, both from Daron, who created the Armenian alphabet. And Vartàn the Great, who is known as the savior of Christianity in Armenia, fought against the Persian hordes who were imposing Zoroastrianism on the Armenians. So we associate the word Daron with fighters. This soup is also known as the Brave Man's Soup. Now when we know the value of vitamins and strength-giving foods, we realize what a great deal of nutritional value this barley soup has.

I also want to call attention to its similarity to Scotch Barley Broth. I don't claim to be an historian or an archaeologist, but I do know you can trace people's origins through their ways of preparing foods. I am convinced that the Scotch people migrated from the Balkans or the Caucasian plateau. It is seen not only in the similarity of these soups, but in their clothes, with skirts and leather bags hanging from their belts, and in their bagpipes. A bagpipe is the instrument of every shepherd in the mountains of Armenia. I go even further and claim that the English plum pudding is not native to Scotland, but was taken there from Corinthia, or from the Isles of Greece. You will see the similarity when we come to desserts. But now, back to Daron Abour.

1 gallon broth (lamb, beef, or chicken)
1 cup pearl barley
2 large onions chopped very fine
1 cup butter
parsley and mint
grated carrots to add color and food value

To prepare this soup, have on hand broth of chicken, beef, or lamb. (You have a good friend in your butcher—always ask him for the bones to use for broth.)

Cook all ingredients together until barley is soft. Season with salt and pepper. The gallon of broth will cook down to about ¾ gallon when soup is done.

ISHKEMBA CHORBA
Tripe Soup

Tripe soup deserves a monument erected in its honor in Constantinople, because that city has made Ishkemba Chorba famous, and vice versa. In all my travels I have never come across anything (except perhaps the hot dog stand in America) that has given so much emphasis to a food as has been given to tripe soup in that famous old capital. In the business sections, or at the gates to bazaars, you always find a stand with a great big kettle built on a tile platform, and with a fire going underneath. You not only get its aroma a block away (of the garlic, not the tripe, however), but you hear the rhythmic tap-tap of the master chorba maker as he expertly chops the tripe.

As you get nearer, if you have any inclination toward being a gourmet or just appreciate good food, you cannot resist entering that little soup stand. It is crowded every hour of the day. You may be sitting alongside a *hamal,* a human pack animal who carries loads of 500 to 600 pounds all day long. Or you must watch your manners, for you may be sitting alongside the pasha himself. Democracy never existed in my day in Turkey, except in these soup stands.

To make Ishkemba Chorba, use:

2 pounds tripe	2 lemons
1 gallon water	2 eggs
2 cloves of garlic	salt and pepper

Boil clean tripe for 3 hours with finely chopped garlic. Put tripe through a meat grinder or chop fine, then return to soup stock and cook for 10 minutes. Beat eggs thoroughly, adding lemon juice while beating. Gradually add some broth to the egg and lemon, pouring it on slowly so that it will not curdle. That is your thickening and your flavoring. Combine this with remaining soup and serve with paprika-butter topping each bowl. To make paprika-butter, cream butter with paprika and put a very little in each bowl. It spreads over the top and makes a lovely pink coloring.

HAVABOUR
Wedding Soup

Wedding soup is simply broth, usually chicken, with boiled vermicelli added. It is then mixed with lemon and egg, as in the tripe soup above. It is served at ceremonial dinners. Usually, as the wedding party arrives, it is mixed and served at once.

½ gallon chicken broth
1 cupful fine vermicelli
3 eggs, raw
juice of 2 lemons
salt and pepper

Cook vermicelli in broth; add beaten egg and lemon juice as in tripe soup.

TAAN ABOUR

1 cup pearl barley
6 cupfuls broth
4 cupfuls madzoon
¼ pound butter
1 cupful chopped onions
½ cupful chopped parsley and mint
salt and pepper

Soak barley overnight. Cook in broth. Sauté onions in butter and pour into barley and broth. Add mint, parsley, and seasonings. Cook for 1½ hours. When barley is tender, add well-beaten madzoon and cook for 5 minutes longer. Serve at once. The leftover soup may be served cold the following day. This is a very nutritious soup.

VOSP ABOUR
Lentil Soup

1 gallon beef or lamb broth
½ pound dried lentils
1 large onion
¼ cupful finely chopped parsley
6 leaves of fresh mint chopped fine
½ cupful butter
salt and pepper

Soak lentils overnight in cold water. Pour off water and add soaked lentils to soup stock. Simmer for 2 hours with onion that is browned in butter, and add salt and pepper. Add mint and parsley during the last 10 minutes. If you like wine flavoring, add a teaspoonful of sherry to each bowl of soup when serving.

CHICKEN SOUP

To make chicken soup, first make a simple chicken broth by simmering a 4-pound chicken in 1 gallon of water. For this purpose I prefer unflavored broth. By putting in vegetables, such as onion, tomatoes, and celery, you detract from the flavor of the bird.

½ gallon chicken broth

⅔ cupful chopped celery

½ cupful uncooked rice

salt and pepper

1 cupful diced chicken meat

Cook celery in broth until half done. Add rice and seasoning and simmer until rice is cooked. Add diced chicken just before serving.

SPLIT PEA SOUP

1 gallon broth (lamb, beef, or chicken)

2 cupfuls dry split peas

1 large carrot

1 branch of celery

1 cupful sliced onion

1 cupful milk

2 tablespoonfuls flour

½ cupful butter

salt and pepper

Soak peas overnight. Boil in soup stock with carrots and celery. Sauté onions in butter and pour into stock. Simmer all together for 2 hours. Then beat flour in milk and add to stock. Put the whole thing through a sieve and serve very hot.

CLAM CHOWDER

1 cupful chopped clams, fresh or canned
2 slices bacon
1 cube butter
1 cupful chopped celery
1 cupful chopped onions
2 cupfuls diced potatoes
½ cupful tomato sauce or purée
½ gallon water or broth
salt and pepper to taste

Put celery, clams, and tomato purée into soup stock or water and simmer for 45 minutes. Sauté chopped bacon until lightly browned, then add butter and onions. Sauté these together until onions are tender. Add to soup stock and cook slowly for another hour. Last, add the potatoes and seasonings and cook until done. The whole process should take about 2½ hours, and you then have a delicious chowder.

ONION SOUP

We always think of onion soup in connection with French restaurants, and rarely think of preparing it at home. It seems to be a sort of monopoly of the French, yet onion soup is one of the oldest soups in the world and is eaten by all peoples, because the onion is grown in nearly all parts of the world.

To make good onion soup, you must have good broth, lots of onions, and lots of time for cooking. Onion soup should cook for at least 6 hours on a slow fire. It is preferable to start it in the morning and let it simmer all day for serving that night.

  1 cube butter

  1 pound onions sliced very fine or chopped

  ½ gallon broth or soup stock

  salt and pepper

Melt butter in soup pot and braise onions well. Add broth and seasonings and simmer on slow fire for not less than 3 hours, and preferably longer. Some people like to give this soup "a French touch" by adding grated cheese, but why disguise the onion flavor?

ARMIENSKY BORSCH

This soup differs from the Russian borsch in that Armenians use more vegetables. They use grated carrots, celery, onions, beets, and cabbage. The vegetables are braised in butter, and simmered in broth. Beets are cooked separately with skins on, then skinned and chopped and added at the last minute in order to keep the fresh red color. They lose color and flavor if they are cooked in the raw soup.

In order to live up to the "sky" ending of the Armenian borsch, you put smetana, or sour cream, on top of each serving. If you like tartness in soup, wash well a whole lemon, then poke holes in it and drop it into the soup pot whole. When soup is cooked, remove lemon and throw it away. If you don't care for lemon juice, try substituting fresh sauerkraut for the cabbage in your Armiensky borsch.

    ½ cupful butter
    ½ cupful chopped onions
    ½ cupful chopped carrots
    ½ cupful chopped celery
    2 cupfuls finely sliced cabbage
    1 cupful chopped beets
    salt and pepper
    ½ gallon soup stock or plain water

Combine as indicated above.

Salads

Our first specialty in this section is potato salad. Yes, that is right. It may seem surprising that of all the attractive salads there are, I have chosen potato salad. The story goes back twenty odd years.

I arrived in New York in the month of July, in 1922, and got on one of those trains that took eight days to get to San Francisco. People could see that I couldn't speak English because I was labeled with a tag showing my name and destination. Fortunately, my brother had sent me money enough so that I could well afford to eat in the dining car, but the trouble was that I couldn't order in English. Being able to read French, I could make out potato salad on the menu. It is practically the same in my language, so I took a chance and ordered it for my first dinner. The next day I was presented with an identical menu. Again I ordered potato salad. This went on for eight days, and it was *bad* potato salad—really terrible potato salad.

Right then and there I resolved that some day when I got the opportunity I was going to serve to Americans the best potato salad in the world. And that is the reason why, in my sandwich shops today, I serve more than a thousand orders of potato salad a day. It is the same potato salad that I serve at outstanding functions. I use it not only as a fine delicacy, but for buffet luncheons I use a large plateful as the table centerpiece, with the message of the day written on it in colored mayonnaise.

POTATO SALAD

1 pound firm, fresh potatoes

2 hardboiled eggs

1 teaspoonful salt

white pepper to taste

¼ cupful vinegar

1 pimiento (chopped fine)

⅔ cupful mayonnaise

1 small onion sliced

2 tablespoonfuls chopped parsley

Boil potatoes in skins. When cool, peel and cut in quarters. Then slice or dice. Add vinegar, mix well, and let soak. Slice onion, and pour salt over it. Then squeeze out all the juice, and wash salt away with cold water. Mix onion with potatoes; add pimiento, eggs, salt and pepper, parsley and mayonnaise. Mix well and let stand in refrigerator for some time before serving.

IMMIGRANT'S PACK SALAD
Raw Spinach Salad

Not only has this salad made me famous, but I can truthfully say that it has become the sensation of the country. The reason is that no one can believe that raw spinach can taste as good as this does.

This salad is called Immigrant's Pack because when I served it for the Wine and Food Society, I packed the spinach in pickled cabbage leaves and made a bum's pack with a bread stick for a handle. I thought of this name, because this was the only pack I had when I started in business. I couldn't speak the language of this wonderful land, but one of my first creations to catch on with the American public was this salad.

Who would ever think that this lowly spinach, most despised of all vegetables by many children and grownups, would some day be served on gold platters, as it was at the Jonathan Club in Los Angeles at a famous gourmets' dinner.

To make it: Remove stems from raw spinach. Wash very well in cold water. To help remove sand and grit, add 1 teaspoon of baking soda to the water in which you wash it. Drain spinach well and cut into strips 1 inch wide. Season with salad oil and lemon juice, and chill. When ready to serve, add hardboiled eggs (chopped) and garnish with tomatoes and asparagus. Serve with the following dressing.

OMAR'S DRESSING

2 eggs

1 tablespoonful sugar

1 teaspoonful salt

½ teaspoonful paprika

½ teaspoonful dry mustard

1 teaspoonful Worcestershire sauce

½ cupful catsup

1 pint salad oil

½ cupful vinegar

⅔ cupful warm water

Mix all ingredients except oil, vinegar, and water in mixing bowl that has been rubbed with garlic clove. Stir them into a smooth paste. Add oil slowly, alternating with vinegar. Beat in electric mixer into a thick dressing, adding the warm water slowly. Keep in a cool place.

HAIGAGAN SALAD
Rudy Vallee Special

1 head of lettuce, cut in cubes
2 tomatoes, peeled and cut in eighths
1 cucumber, halved and sliced
½ cupful chopped parsley
⅓ cupful oil
⅓ cupful vinegar
salt and pepper

Mix cut vegetables lightly in bowl. Add salt, pepper, oil, and vinegar. Toss to mix, and serve in attractive individual bowls, or on salad plates.

CELERY ROOT SALAD

2 large celery roots
1 onion, parsley, 2 bay leaves
salt and pepper

Peel celery root, and boil in a pot of stock or plain water to which cut-up onions, whole parsley, bay leaves, salt and pepper have been added. When tender, remove from pot and slice in small pieces, as in potato salad. Serve with this dressing:

1 cupful oil (olive or peanut)
1 cupful vinegar (tarragon)
⅓ teaspoonful mustard
½ teaspoonful salt
¼ teaspoonful freshly ground black pepper

Mix all together and pour over sliced celery root while it is still hot, so that dressing will soak into vegetable. Chill and serve on lettuce leaves.

KHOROVADZ SEMPOOG AGHTZAN
Eggplant Caviar

1 eggplant
3 tomatoes
2 tablespoonfuls chopped onion
2 tablespoonfuls chopped parsley
3 tablespoonfuls oil
3 tablespoonfuls vinegar
salt and pepper

Bake or broil a whole large eggplant until soft. When broiled under open gas fire, it will burn outer skin, but eggplant will have a delicious smoked flavor. Let cool, then peel off browned or burned skin. Chop moderately fine. Add chopped onions and parsley. Season with oil, vinegar, salt, pepper, and mix well. Serve on lettuce leaf with olive in center; garnish with sliced tomato.

ROMAINE SALAD À LA OMAR

2 heads romaine lettuce
½ cupful mayonnaise
½ cupful catsup
2 tablespoonfuls vinegar
1 teaspoonful Worcestershire sauce
½ teaspoonful salt
dash of pepper
1 chopped hardboiled egg

Lay romaine leaves on flat salad plates. Mix mayonnaise, adding balance of ingredients, into a smooth dressing. Pour over romaine and sprinkle top with chopped eggs and paprika. Serve.

SAN FRANCISCO CRAB LOUIS

Visitors in San Francisco usually ask for fresh crabs, and Crab Louis, as it has been developed in this city, is a favorite delicacy of gourmets. Here is a simple recipe for making it.

> 1 pound crab meat (2 large fresh crabs)
> 1 large head lettuce, shredded
> salt and pepper

Mix shredded crab and lettuce, saving crab legs to put on top of salad after dressing has been poured on.

DRESSING:

> ½ cupful mayonnaise
> 1 cupful chili sauce (tomato sauce or catsup can be used)
> 6 ripe olives chopped fine
> 4 small sweet pickles chopped
> 1 tablespoonful chopped parsley
> 1 teaspoonful Worcestershire sauce

Mix ingredients well to make a fine smooth dressing. Chill in refrigerator. When ready to serve, see that dressing covers the whole bed of mixed crab and lettuce. Top with crab legs. Garnish with quartered lemons.

CRANBERRY SALAD
or
MEAT GARNISH

> 1 pound cranberries
> 1 package marshmallows (16)
> 1 cupful sugar
> 1 orange

Put cranberries and whole orange with peel through medium cutter of meat grinder. Mix in sugar. Cut marshmallows into small pieces with scissors and mix with other ingredients. This makes a tart sauce to serve with meats, or is delicious as a light salad. It will keep for some time in the refrigerator, and improves in flavor as it stands.

NOTE: Dip scissors in water before cutting marshmallows, and they will not stick to the blades.

RAQUEL TORRES SALAD

2 avocados
2 tomatoes
2 teaspoonfuls finely chopped onion
2 tablespoonfuls chopped pickled peppers
2 tablespoonfuls vinegar or lemon juice
salt and pepper

Cut avocados into small cubes. Peel and cut up tomatoes. Chop peppers. Mix all together with salt, pepper, and vinegar. Serve on crisp lettuce. Or mash ingredients and serve on crackers for hors d'oeuvres.

KIDNEY or WHITE BEAN SALAD

½ pound boiled white or kidney beans
1 large onion
¼ cupful parsley, chopped fine
3 tablespoonfuls olive, peanut, or salad oil
3 tablespoonfuls vinegar or lemon
salt and pepper

Mix beans, sliced onions, parsley, oil, vinegar, salt and pepper. Serve on crisp lettuce leaves; garnish with tomato and olives.

NOTE: In order to get quick results in cooking the beans,

follow this method. Boil beans for 30 minutes, add 2 teaspoonfuls soda, and boil for 10 minutes more. Strain off water, add
fresh hot water and boil for 30 minutes. Although soda takes
away some of the food value, it helps to eliminate gas effect.

COLE SLAW

3 cupfuls finely chopped cabbage
2 cooked beets
1 bell pepper
1 cupful mayonnaise
½ cupful vinegar
2 tablespoonfuls sugar
salt and pepper

Chop cabbage very fine. Add sugar and vinegar and let stand
for at least an hour. Try to squeeze all water out of cabbage,
then wash with cold water and drain. Add chopped beets and
thinly shredded bell pepper, cut in strips about 1 inch long.
Season and mix with mayonnaise.

VI

Eggs

Eggs are an essential food, and this country has been blessed with such a supply of them that if every person ate two eggs a day, there would still be plenty.

I know of no other food that can be used for as many purposes as eggs. They can be served in one form or another for any meal, and they are also an indispensable cooking ingredient. What would we use if we didn't have them for thickening sauces, for pie fillings, soups, custards, and dressings? They are the source of leavening when we use them in soufflés, cakes, and omelettes. Eggs are used for coating when we fry cutlets, croquettes, fish, breaded chops, and steaks. For breads, muffins, cookies, croquettes, and meat balls we use eggs as a binder to hold other ingredients together. Eggs improve the texture of frozen mixtures, because they act as a sort of wrapper around each crystal of sugar, and so prevent lumping. Eggs are used also as a clarifier of broths and bouillon. They give life to dressings. Without them we could have no hollandaise, mayonnaise and other fine salad dressings. As a garnish for salads, cold meats, and shellfish, they are indispensable. In short, eggs are the foundation of a good cuisine.

Ceremonial soups in Armenia are never served without the lemon-egg dressing. Besides adding food value, this dressing has a symbolic meaning for religious festivities. Long before Christianity, the Hebrews, Assyrians, Egyptians, Persians, Greeks, Romans, Armenians, and all the people living in the cradle of civilization used eggs on occasions of pomp and ceremony. To them, the egg symbolized the Universe, and was presented to their gods as an offering. The outer shell represented the limitless sky, and the inner skin the air. The white of the egg was the waters, and the yolk was the earth. Starting early in the Christian era, the symbol of coloring eggs at Easter time meant that the salvation of the world was bought with the blood of Christ.

In the last war, my buddy and captain was very fond of eggs. When we entered a captured town it was my difficult job, as unofficial cook of our outfit, to find eggs and fix him an omelette. I still treasure the last letter he wrote to me just before he was shot. He was trying to lure me back to Armenia. "Forget everything, and come back," he wrote, "as eggs are now very plentiful."

Here's a tip for singers! My mother used to make me drink a raw egg to make my voice better when I was singing as a choir boy. Try it. It helps.

HAM AND EGGS OMAR

We will start with Ham and Eggs Omar, one of the most often requested dishes in my restaurant. There is a secret to making even ham and eggs come out just right. Mine is to use plenty of butter, an ample amount of thinly sliced, well-cured ham, and to bake the eggs in the oven covered, so that they steam.

Melt 2 pats of butter in an individual casserole. Put in 2 or 3 slices of thinly cut ham to cover bottom. Break eggs on a saucer and slide them onto ham. Bake in oven, covered, until eggs are pinky-white on top. When the cover is lifted, a delicious aroma arises and the eggs smile up at you. No seasoning should be used until eggs are served at the table.

POACHED EGGS VIENNA STYLE

The reason for giving this recipe is to warn readers that when you see "Vienna style" on the menu, this dish is no different from any eggs poached in milk or cream, and served with strips of bacon on top. But on account of the fancy name, you pay a fancy price. It is as easy as this to make. For individual servings, use:

1 cupful milk or thin cream
2 eggs
3 slices bacon
2 slices buttered toast

Bring milk to boil, and poach eggs in the milk. Have buttered toast ready on plate. Lift eggs carefully and place on toast. Pour hot milk over to soak into toast. Have bacon fried very crisp, and place on eggs, one strip in the center, and one on each side. It makes a pretty and nutritious dish.

SCRAMBLED EGGS

Probably more eggs are cooked by this method than any other, for it is easiest when serving crowds. Breakfast clubs everywhere serve them with ham or bacon, and some of them are pretty bad.

Now why put such a delicate dish as scrambled eggs in the category of bad food when, with only a little attention, one can make a nice, fluffy, sunshiny dish that will appeal to any gourmet? For eggs are the favorite food of many of the world's great personalities, among them President Roosevelt.

To make scrambled eggs perfectly: Melt plenty of butter in a pre-heated frying pan. (Be sure that the pan is well scoured so that eggs will come out golden in color, and untainted in flavor.)

For each person, beat 2 eggs with 3 tablespoonfuls of cream. Salt and pepper to taste. Beat very well, and pour into hot butter in pan. Stir constantly while cooking. The eggs should cook only about a minute, or until just set. Be sure the plate on which they are to be served is good and hot. There is nothing more objectionable than cold eggs.

SCRAMBLED EGGS WITH FRESH TOMATOES

Here is the perfect dish for those in search of an effective, natural laxative. It is a favorite Near East breakfast. Use 1 tomato and 2 eggs per person. Peel and chop tomato. Sauté in pure butter, and add salt and pepper. Break eggs directly into the tomatoes and stir constantly while cooking. The eggs will set in about 1 minute.

BAKED CHEESE or HAM OMELETTE

Omelettes are the crowning achievement of a good egg chef. They are very simple to make if you observe certain rules. (1) Eggs must be well beaten. (2) Pan or casserole must be well buttered and hot when eggs are put in. (3) Oven must be at proper temperature, 375 degrees. (4) Always serve omelette immediately after it comes from the oven, and on very hot plates. For 4 people, use:

   6 eggs
   ¼ pound cheese (American) cut in small cubes, or
   ¼ pound ham diced
   ⅛ pound butter
    salt and pepper

Melt butter in casserole. See that sides are well buttered. Beat eggs well until fluffy and light. Fold in cheese or ham and seasonings. Pour into hot casserole and bake for about 15 minutes, or until light and well set. Serve at once. Chopped parsley makes an interesting variation to this dish, and provides a rich source of vitamins.

HAIGAGAN OMELETTE
Armenian Omelette

This is an excellent way to cook eggs when you wish to prepare a large quantity. Plan to use 1½ eggs per person. To serve 4 people, use:

6 eggs

1 bell pepper

2 large fresh tomatoes, peeled and cut up

½ onion, chopped fine (optional)

¼ pound boiled salami, chopped fine

½ cube butter

½ teaspoonful salt

Fry the finely chopped pepper and onion. Then add tomatoes and cook for 5 minutes. Add chopped salami, and heat thoroughly. Butter bottom of baking pan (a square cake pan is excellent). Beat the eggs and mix well with the tomato mixture. Bake in hot oven for 5 to 10 minutes, or until eggs are set and slightly brown on top. Cut in squares and serve immediately on very hot plates. This is a perfect dish for large parties or Sunday suppers. We serve it often for Armenian wedding breakfasts in Fresno.

FILLED OMELETTES
Asparagus, Oyster, Crab, or Shrimp

Make a thick, well-seasoned cream sauce, and add asparagus or shellfish. While this is cooking, beat eggs (using 2 eggs per person) and pour into a hot buttered pan. Flop eggs over to cook both sides. Add 3 tablespoonfuls of the cream filling and roll up individual omelettes. You can cook this type omelette a little browner than you would normally cook eggs, because of the cream filling.

SPINACH AND EGGS

Here is a simple, delicious, and nourishing luncheon dish. Fry cooked, seasoned spinach in butter. Leftover spinach is excellent for this. Put in individual baking dishes. Break 2 eggs over the top, and bake, covered, in a hot oven until eggs are set and the flavors blended.

EGG SALAD WITH ROMAINE

These foods seem to have a natural affinity for each other and make a perfect combination.

Boil eggs until hard. Chill and cut into eighths. Place on top of romaine lettuce. Pour oil around generously, salt and pepper, and squeeze lemon juice over all. This makes the perfect dressing for eggs.

DZIRANOV HAVGIT
Eggs with Apricots

For the last egg recipe, I have saved my most exotic egg dish. You will like it.

Apricots came originally from Armenia. In the hot valleys in summer you can smell the delicious aroma of the fruit as it is being strung into leis for drying, and as it is being cooked and preserved. The fruit in the Old Country seems to have been much more fragrant than the apricots in California.

Try this apricot omelette and you will serve it often as a main dish for luncheon, or for informal suppers.

    6 eggs
    1 large can apricots, or
    2 cupfuls cooked, dried apricots
    ¼ cupful butter

Drain off juice and put apricots through a sieve. Pour pulp into pre-heated butter, and simmer. Beat eggs thoroughly and add to apricots, stirring constantly so that eggs will not lump. Serve at once on hot plates with rice pilaff.

VII

Fish

HAVING grown up in seaports on the shores of the Bosporus, I am very partial to sea food. Every time I think of fish, it reminds me of the days when as a boy I witnessed the generosity of the fishermen in Constantinople. There, all fishermen are either Armenian or Greek. No other land has such fascinating and picturesque fishermen. They are the happy-go-lucky people of the country. They have hearts as big as the sea in which they fish. They are as crude as their hands become in handling fish; and they are as strong as some of the catch they take.

Twice a year there is a very big run of fish—two different species in two extremes of size. One is very small like our silver smelts, and the other is very much like our bonita, but not quite so large. The small ones are called *khamsi;* the large ones *palamoud.*

The palamoud is a Black Sea product. It swims down from the Black Sea to the Bosporus and Marmora Sea in great quantities in late fall. Some days they swarm in such tremendous schools that they are actually thrown up on the shores by the waves. Then the fishermen roll up their wide, bell-bottomed pants and go to work gathering up the fish and piling them on huge wooden trays. Balancing the trays on their heads, they distribute the fish to the poor all over the city. That is the one day the fisherman refuses to accept pay. No rich man can buy any of the fish, for it is their firm belief that this is a gift from God sent for the poor alone.

In the early spring, with the coming of the south wind, which is called *lodos,* there are runs of the little silver smelt. By thousands they swarm around the shores. You don't have to go to the bazaars, or the fish markets, or wait for the fishermen to come to your door to know that the khamsi are running. The smell of fish being broiled over outdoor charcoal burners and the smoke hanging over the city will tell you. Everybody has set up his *manghal,* or stove, outdoors in order to keep the smell out of the house.

The method these people use to broil fish can be applied to our inland trout or to any small fish that come from the sea.

I believe San Francisco is destined to become one of the finest sea-food centers in the world, because of its closeness to Monterey Bay. Here, ichthyologists tell us, are to be found more kinds of fish than in any other bay in the world. Of course I have my doubts, because I don't see how any place could have more varieties than you get around the Marmora and the Aegean Archipelago. I won't argue with the scientists about this, but I will argue about the relative values of our ways of cooking fish. Armenians don't wrap it up in paper and cream it and pour on fancy sauces that destroy the delicate flavor. They simply put it on a griddle with pure butter or olive oil and cook it. When you eat it, you have the crispy, crusty outside, and a flaky, delicate, white meat inside, seasoned only with the juice of lemons grown under a brilliant sun.

The most famous fish in northern California waters is the sandab, equivalent to the pompano of the East Coast and of New Orleans. When eating this delicacy, please do not insult this creation of the gods by dunking it in tartar sauce or similar embellishments. Serve it simply. Above all, buy firm, fresh fish. You can always tell fresh fish by opening the ear. If blood is bright red, fish is good; if dark red, the fish is apt to be old. Cook it as follows:

SANDABS

sandabs
1 egg
1 cupful milk
salt and pepper
flour

Add milk to beaten egg and mix well. Dip fish in mixture, and roll in flour. (Cornmeal and breadcrumbs are suitable only for larger fish.) Fry rather slowly in hot butter or oil until golden brown, and serve with lemon slices. It is as easy as that!

Being at heart a fisherman, I must tell how fish are caught around Lake Sevan, high in the heart of the Caucasian mountains, about 20 miles from Erivan, the capital of Armenia. This is undoubtedly the coldest and deepest lake in the region, with a deep hidden spring at its bottom. Irrigation streams reach down into the valleys in all directions, and at each of these outlets you will see fishermen, naked to the waist, spearing fish on long bamboo poles. The big beauties in this lake are so plentiful, and the water is so clear, that a skilled fisherman can toss them out as fast as he can get his hook back into the water. This fish is called *ishkhana tzoog*, or prince fish. It is a variety of spotted trout similar to our rainbow trout, and is so rich in oil that it can be simply broiled and eaten with salt and pepper.

BROILED TROUT

Keep a sauce for broiling fish always on hand. Make it as follows: Chop 1 whole garlic clove finely and add it to 1 cup olive oil. Keep in covered jar. When ready to broil your trout, add 1 teaspoonful of this garlic oil to 2 tablespoonfuls of olive or salad oil. Add a dash of salt, pepper, and paprika, and brush over cleaned fish.

Wash and clean trout well; cut off the fins, but leave head and tail on. Wipe dry and brush with above sauce. Place on grill and broil slowly over charcoal about 6 inches from the coals. You can get a small portable broiler for a few dollars that will prove to be worth its weight in gold, for it is fun to use, and simplifies cooking. Be sure to keep the window open when using a charcoal broiler indoors, for unpleasant and noxious fumes are given off. Serve broiled trout with lemon dressing made as follows:

LEMON DRESSING WITH PIAZ

Piaz is an onion and parsley mixture. Slice onion thin and let it stand in plenty of salt. Squeeze out the juice, rinse in cold water, and chop a generous amount of parsley. Add both to lemon juice and mix well.

NOTE: If you don't care for broiled trout, cook it the same way as the sandabs.

BOUILLABAISSE À LA MARSEILLES

1 4-pound red fish, red snapper, or trout (halibut or barracuda)
2 cloves garlic
½ pound prawns
4 tomatoes
2 dozen oysters or mussels
1 tablespoonful parsley
3 onions
½ cupful olive oil
1 pinch saffron
salt and pepper to taste

Put the olive oil in a saucepan, add chopped tomatoes, onions, garlic, and parsley. Let all this simmer, then throw a good pinch of saffron in and season with salt and pepper to taste. Now put in prawns. Cook for 15 minutes. Then add sliced fish and let boil for another 15 minutes. Add oysters and cook for 10 minutes more. The pan must be covered during all this operation. Sprinkle the purée and ingredients with parsley. Serve on slices of toasted French bread.

FISH PLAKI

2 pounds bass, barracuda, fresh tuna, or halibut

2 slices onion

⅓ cupful chopped parsley

1 clove garlic (optional)

1 can solid pack tomatoes, or

4 large fresh tomatoes

1 large potato, cubed

4 cupfuls water

2 teaspoonfuls peanut or olive oil

salt and pepper

Cut the 2 pounds of fish into 6 pieces for individual servings. Put in pot with oil, onions, parsley, garlic, tomatoes, potatoes, salt, and pepper. Add water and cover pot. Cook for 1 hour. Serve either hot or cold in stew bowls.

SGOUMRI DOLMA
Stuffed Baby Mackerel or Bonita

It is important that fish for baking should be strictly fresh so that it will not fall to pieces. Clean mackerel or bonita carefully, without making a cut in the belly. Clean opening in the neck, and break spine at both ends. Then roll fish back and forth on board to loosen flesh. When loosened, take hold of spine at neck end; it should pull out easily. Remove all loose flesh, chop it, and mix with stuffing.

STUFFING:

2 onions chopped fine

1 carrot chopped

2 tablespoonfuls pine nuts

¼ teaspoonful allspice

¼ teaspoonful cinnamon

Mix well with fish particles, and stuff into cavity. Dip in batter made with egg, milk, and flour, and fry in oil until golden brown. This is delicious served cold and sliced.

BOILED FISH WITH WINE SAUCE

4 pieces of fish (serving size—⅓ pound halibut, bass, filet of sole may be used)

⅓ cube butter

2 tablespoonfuls flour

1 cupful milk

½ cupful dry white wine

salt and pepper

⅓ teaspoonful allspice

Boil fish with allspice for 25 minutes. While fish is boiling, melt butter in a saucepan and add flour. Brown it lightly, season with salt and pepper, and add milk and wine to make smooth sauce. Put through a sieve so that there are no lumps in it. Pour sauce in bottom of platter and put boiled fish on top. Sprinkle generously with parsley and serve with boiled or mashed potatoes.

BOILED STRIPED BASS

Boil fish until tender. Take out bones, and break up into large flakes. Make a rich cream sauce, and add to fish. Put into buttered casserole, with breadcrumbs, butter, and paprika on top. Bake until lightly browned, and serve very hot.

BAKED STRIPED BASS

Clean fish and place in baking pan with sliced tomatoes, slices of lemon, and some of the garlic-oil sauce, according to taste. Salt, pepper, and sprinkle with paprika. Bake in moderate oven for 1 hour. When serving, sprinkle with chopped parsley.

STEAMED FISH

Parboil sliced carrots, celery, and parsley, and a very little garlic. Use no onions. Place large cuts of fish on bed of vegetables. Add salt, pepper, and oil. Cover tightly and cook over slow fire on top of stove for about 45 minutes.

FRIED FISH

Have peanut oil or olive oil very hot. Dip fish in flour and fry both sides until light golden brown. Do not put butter on fish. Serve with kidney bean salad.

VIII

Bread

BREAD is the most important item in an Armenian's life, not only because he has been deprived of other foods for six hundred years and has been compelled to thrive on bread, but also because it is considered a sacred product. No bread crumb falls to the ground in the presence of an Armenian, and goes unnoticed. He will immediately pick it up, kiss it, and say a prayer. Then he will place it on a wall for the birds to eat.

Breaking bread is a ceremonial custom, and a sign of hospitality in every Armenian household. And since every Armenian housewife must make her own bread, she has naturally found ways to shorten this daily labor. So, in years of experimenting, Armenian women have evolved lavash. This is a flat, round bread that can be kept a month without becoming moldy, and without losing its freshness. Although it looks like matzoth it differs a great deal from them because lavash has both leavening and salt, while matzoth have neither. Lavash in Armenia is cooked in an oven in the ground, or in the floor of the house. A pit is lined with bricks and the fire is laid directly on that. You must remove the coals before you put your bread in to bake. But in this country, with modern electrical and gas stoves, the operation is greatly simplified, so try the following recipe in your own oven.

LAVASH

3 pounds all-purpose flour
1 yeast cake
2 teaspoonfuls salt
lukewarm water to make a stiff dough

Dissolve yeast cake in 2 cups of warm water. Sift flour and salt into a large bowl. Make a depression in the center of the flour and gradually work in dissolved yeast cake and enough water to make a stiff dough. Knead well, place in bowl, cover, and let stand for about 3 hours. Punch dough down and let rise again.

Sift flour over a large board or table top, and spread evenly over surface. Now pinch off pieces of dough about the size of a large egg. With a long rolling pin (like a broomstick) roll dough out into a large sheet, as large as your oven will accommodate. Dough should be about ⅛ inch thick. Place on a cookie sheet, or the bottom of the oven, and bake at 400 degrees for about 3 minutes. Then place under broiler to brown the top lightly, watching all the time to keep from burning.

Repeat this process until all the dough has been used up. Store in a dry place and use as needed.

To make sandwiches of lavash: Sprinkle water on both sides, and put in the desired filling. Then wrap in a towel for a few minutes before serving. Or spread the moistened lavash with a Bertouge cheese-and-parsley filling and roll up like Mexican tacos.

PEDA BREAD

Peda bread is the most popular Armenian bread in America. It is sold in all centers where Armenians gather. Peda, to me, tastes better during the Mohammedan Ramadan. That is the season when all Mohammedans observe 40 days of fasting during the hours when the sun is up. Even here in California I have had a chance to watch Egyptian and Arabian students from the International House in Berkeley enjoy breaking their fast. They fast all day, and then come to my restaurant to eat fresh peda bread and other native foods. This is the time when freshly baked peda bread tastes wonderful. It is sometimes called dunking bread, for it is so good when soaked up with meat and vegetable juices.

6 cupfuls flour
1 cupful milk or water
2 tablespoonfuls shortening or butter
1 tablespoonful salt
2 tablespoonfuls sugar
1 yeast cake
½ cupful lukewarm water

Dissolve yeast in lukewarm water. Warm the milk and add to it the sugar, melted shortening, and salt. Sift flour into a large bowl and work into it the liquids until it reaches the consistency of bread dough. Let rise, covered with a damp towel, for 2 hours. Remove to floured board and knead down. Cover again and let rise for about an hour.

Now pinch off pieces the size of a lemon. Roll out to oblong pieces ½ inch thick. Place side by side in a baking pan. You can make the loaves any size or shape you like, for individual or larger servings. Brush top of bread with butter. Bake in a 400-degree oven for 10 minutes, and then lower the heat to 350 degrees. Bake until nicely browned all over. Serve hot. This bread may be reheated in the oven for later use.

GATAH

Gatah is the favorite breakfast or tea bread. An Armenian may forget his mother tongue, he may forget everything about his native land, but he will never forget his mother's gatahs. In most cases, gatahs are like firm rolls sprinkled with sesame seed.

They are delicious with tea, coffee, or any hot beverage, and are especially recommended for afternoon snacks with cheese.

HYASTANI GATAH

1 cupful pure melted butter

4 eggs

1 yeast cake

1 cupful sour cream or madzoon

1 teaspoonful salt

9 cupfuls flour

3 cupfuls lukewarm water

½ cupful sesame seeds

Beat butter well until it is creamy. Add beaten eggs, and yeast that has been dissolved in warm water. Beat these well into the butter, then add sour cream (or madzoon) and the salt. Mix well. Then gradually beat in flour and water to make a stiff dough. This mixing process should take about 15 minutes.

Now take out a handful of dough and put it on a floured board or table. Beat the piece of dough against the table until it is very stringy, then place it in a large bowl. Repeat this until all the dough has been beaten. Then cover the bowl with a cloth and let the dough set until it rises—about 3 hours. To know the readiness of the dough you must recognize the aroma, or when you touch it with your hand it says, "I am ready."

When your gatah dough is ready, take out a piece about the size of a large apple. Roll it out *very* thin with your long rolling pin, as far as it will go without breaking. Brush it with melted butter or peanut oil. Fold up like a handkerchief into packages, brushing each fold with butter. In the last fold put ½ cupful of Khoridz stuffing. Make stuffing as follows:

½ cupful creamed butter
1 cupful sugar
3 cupfuls flour

Mix this together with your fingers until it is crumbly. Stuff into the folded dough. When packages are ready, flatten them out with a rolling pin to about 12 x 14 inches square. They should be about 1 inch thick. Then cut them into any shape you like, say about 3-inch squares, or into oblong shapes. Set gatahs in a greased baking pan. Brush the tops with beaten egg yolks, and sprinkle with sesame seed. Bake in a pre-heated oven at 375 degrees for about 40 minutes.

ANAHID'S GATAH

1 cupful butter
1 cupful pastry cream
1 cupful sugar
3 eggs
3 teaspoonfuls baking powder
1 teaspoonful salt
flour to make stiff dough
1 tablespoonful sesame or poppy seed

Mix butter, cream, eggs, and sugar together by beating well. Then add flour that has been sifted with baking powder and salt. Knead into a stiff dough. Let it stand, covered with a cloth, for 20 minutes. Then pinch off pieces the size of an egg, and roll out between your palms like thin bread sticks. Take 3 of these sticks and braid them together. Place in greased baking sheets. Brush lightly with sesame or poppy seeds. Bake at 375 degrees for 15 to 20 minutes, or until nicely browned.

PIROSHKI
Stuffed Rolls

3½ cupfuls flour
1 cake of yeast
1 teaspoonful salt
¾ cupful lukewarm milk
¼ cupful sugar
¼ cupful butter
1 whole egg
2 yolks of eggs

Crumble yeast in lukewarm milk with 1 teaspoonful of sugar. Let stand for a few minutes. Sift flour with salt into a large bowl. Put yeast mixture into the center of the flour. Mix it into the flour just a little and let stand for a few minutes while it begins to "work." Melt butter, add sugar, and cream well. Add this to the dry ingredients, with the beaten egg. Beat thoroughly for about 10 minutes. Cover dough and let rise for 3 hours in a warm place, or in a lukewarm oven. Pinch off pieces of dough and roll out into 4-inch squares. Have board well drenched with flour. Place 2 tablespoonfuls of filling on each square of dough. Fold over and pinch tightly closed into oblong shapes. Brush with beaten egg yolk and bake in 375-degree oven until nicely browned. If you are in a hurry, piroshki may be fried in deep fat.

FILLING:

⅛ pound butter
1 pound ground raw beef
1 large onion finely chopped
2 hardboiled eggs, chopped
salt and pepper

Fry onion in butter, add ground meat, and sauté with onion. Add salt and pepper. Let cool, and mix with chopped eggs.

Serve piroshki with soup. They are particularly good with Russian borsch.

IX

Paste

PASTE is one of the most essential foods in an Armenian's life. Little girls, before they are ten or twelve, learn to help their mothers prepare very fine layers of paste. This is an art that cannot be accomplished overnight. It takes years of experience to be able to spread a layer of paste 5 feet in diameter across the table, roll it over and over again, and do that with 10 or 12 layers, one on top of the other, without the layers sticking together. No woman in the land of Mt. Ararat is considered a good cook unless her pastry layers are paper thin.

One of the most popular pastes, which originated in Babylon, is called lah majoun. Lah majoun is not only a delightful entree but has the distinction of being the food of the elite. Only sheiks of the desert can afford to eat lah majoun as often as they want to. Again, necessity was the mother of invention for this delicacy, because sheiks, traveling through the desert, were unable to carry prepared food with them because of spoilage from heat and lack of refrigeration. They carried their meat on the hoof, lambs and goats marching along with the caravan. When they ran out of these, they killed the camels. They carried also their flour, or in some cases even whole wheat and the pestles with which to grind it. With these ingredients they made lah majoun. As soon as the caravan came to a halt there was great activity. While tents were being pitched, the women made the fire and placed sheet metal over it. Occasionally at big oases they would find ovens ready built in the rocks, but that was not usual. Caravans now carry butter in earthenware jugs full of rock salt to preserve it. A piece of bread dough is used for yeast to start the new batch, and the paste is made from this. I've never known an aroma like the intoxicating aroma of lah majoun being cooked in the open air of the desert.

The Countess Barbara Hutton Haugwitz-Reventlow, now Mrs. Cary Grant, brought her housekeeper and cook all the way up from Santa Monica to San Francisco in order that I might show her how to make lah majoun, since this is one of her favorite dishes.

LAH MAJOUN

5 cupfuls (1½ pounds) unsifted flour (Gold Medal Kitchen Tested)

4 tablespoonfuls melted butter

1½ teaspoonfuls salt

1½ cupfuls lukewarm water

1 cake Fleischmann's yeast (fresh)

Mix flour and salt. Add butter and the yeast, which has been dissolved in ½ cupful lukewarm water, and knead well, adding the remaining water and working the knuckles well down into the dough. Rest, knead, and repeat the process for about 15 minutes, oiling hands slightly with peanut oil when nearly finished to remove dough and to prevent the formation of crust on the rising batter. Cover, and let stand for at least 2 hours in a warm place.

See recipe for meat stuffing on next page.

MEAT STUFFING:

2 pounds lean lamb
2 large green peppers
2 large ripe tomatoes
2½ cupfuls ground onions
1 cupful tightly packed chopped parsley
5 teaspoonfuls salt
3 teaspoonfuls pepper
2 teaspoonfuls cummin
1 teaspoonful garlic salt
1 tablespoonful tomato catsup
1 teaspoonful paprika

Put the meat, peppers, onions and tomatoes through the meat grinder separately, using medium chopper; retain the natural juices. Mix all ingredients in a bowl and set aside.

To cut and roll dough, have enough sifted flour ready to sprinkle on breadboard while working with dough. Cut dough into 4 equal strips and each of these into 8 parts. Knead each of these into a ball and set aside for 10 minutes, covering with towel. Sprinkle a little flour on breadboard and roll out each ball until it is about 5½ inches in diameter. Roll out only 6 at a time and spread with 2 tablespoonfuls of meat mixture immediately before putting into oven. Roll up edges of pastry about ¼ inch to prevent the loss of juices while cooking.

Heat oven to 500 degrees, grease cookie sheet large enough to hold 6 lah majouns, and cook in lower part of oven for 10 minutes or until dough is pink underneath; then raise pan to upper part of oven and continue baking for 3 or 4 minutes to allow meat to become thoroughly done. When cooked, stack one pastry on top of the other in a large pan; do not cover. Grease pan each time it is refilled.

Lah majoun may be eaten immediately or reheated in a hot oven and used next day. Lemon may be served with them.

BANIROV BEUREK

This pastry is the most common in the homes of all Armenians. It is made with thin layers of pastry and butter and a native cheese which is similar to any white jack cheese. Most important item in the pastry is the parsley, which gives a lovely green color to counteract the whiteness of the paste and cheese, and also contains a lot of vitamins.

6 cupfuls flour
1½ cupfuls water
1 teaspoonful salt
1 tablespoonful peanut oil

Mix dough and let it set at room temperature for 1 hour without touching it. Cover dough with a wet towel to keep from drying out. After 1 hour roll out dough and divide into 8 separate balls. Roll each of these flat with cornstarch. You should be able to make a large round sheet about 3 feet in diameter. Cut this into 4 even pieces; each one makes a beurek. On each section place cheese-parsley stuffing and fold dough over to make a package triangular or round in shape. Place in baking pan, pour melted butter over it, and bake in a moderate oven (350 degrees) for 25 minutes.

STUFFING:

2 pounds cheese grated: Monterey, Swiss, or American
2 raw eggs
½ cupful chopped parsley
salt and pepper

Mix well and use as stuffing for dough.

MISOV BEUREK

This paste is made exactly as the preceding recipe, except that it is stuffed with ground meat that has been braised, instead of the cheese and parsley. It is invariably eaten as an entree. Make plenty of it. It is always popular.

STUFFING:

2 pounds ground lamb or beef

4 large onions chopped fine

½ cupful chopped parsley

2 raw eggs

salt and pepper

Braise meat in a little butter, add onions, chopped parsley, salt and pepper, and break in the raw eggs. Mix well and use for stuffing.

SOU BEUREK

4 eggs

1 teaspoonful salt

2 tablespoonfuls oil (peanut oil may be used)

2¼ cupfuls unsifted flour (Gold Medal Kitchen Tested)

⅛ teaspoonful baking powder

½ cupful cornstarch in sifter

Break eggs into mixing bowl and add salt and oil; mix, but do not beat. Add flour, a cup at a time, adding the baking powder with the first cupful, and knead well for 15 minutes, adding more flour if necessary. The dough should be hard and elastic. Sprinkle a little cornstarch on the breadboard, set dough on it and cut into 4 parts, dividing each of these in half. Roll each part into a ball and place in oiled pan, rolling each ball about until it is coated with oil. Cover tightly and let stand an hour.

CHEESE FILLING:

1 pound Armenian, Monterey, or jack cheese, put through
    medium chopper

¼ cupful finely chopped parsley

1 egg

Mix these ingredients together.

Have ready 2 gallons boiling water mixed with a cupful of salt in a wide-topped pan, and a pan of cold water. Water in both pans must be kept respectively boiling and cold. You will also need a large dry dish towel folded twice, and a tea towel. Keep warm in saucepan ½ cupful melted butter.

Roll out the dough in the way described for Paklava, the sheet being not over 15 inches in diameter. Drop each sheet into boiling water, and when completely submerged remove at once with a large spoon and drop into cold water. Squeeze out as much of the water as possible with the tea towel and spread on dry dish towel; cut with knife to fit pan, spread with melted butter (using pastry brush), and place in pan, fitting side strips around, and buttering them in the same way. Repeat until 4 sheets are placed in pan, spread with cheese mixture, and continue above process until last buttered sheet is on top. Cut into 2½ inch squares with a sharp knife, and bake in a 350-degree oven for about 40 minutes. The top and bottom should be pink when done. Serve hot.

MANTI

Manti is an American version of an Oriental paste. Since Armenians love to be first, I suspect they were annoyed to find that the Chinese were the discoverers of macaroni, and through Marco Polo paste was first introduced to the Near East. Armenians tried to make something new of it after it was introduced to them, and manti is the result. It must be served with madzoon.

This is where the Armenian in me enters the picture, because for this dish I use a lot of garlic.

The dough is the same as the Sou Beurek dough, but you roll it out 1/16 inch thick. Then cut into 1-inch squares. Add ¼ teaspoonful of stuffing and fold into a package, pressing the edges of the dough together. Grease a baking pan and place the packages in it, rather close together. Bake in a hot oven until light brown. Drain off the butter that might have accumulated and pour well-seasoned chicken or turkey broth over the squares, adding enough to cover. Bake again for another 20 minutes. Serve hot. These should be served with madzoon seasoned with garlic.

STUFFING:

½ pound lean lamb ground

1 small onion chopped fine

salt and pepper

Cook together in butter until done. Let it get cold before stuffing manti.

SPINACH PASTE

Follow directions for Banirov Beurek, using chopped spinach. We usually add a little cheese to kill the flatness of the spinach, or if you don't care for this combination, braised browned meat and spinach make an interesting combination.

SPINACH STUFFING:

Salt raw spinach leaves and let stand for 1 hour. Squeeze the spinach to soften it, and wash with cold water. Sauté in butter, add salt, pepper, and cheese, and use as stuffing.

MACARONI CHEESE PASTE

This is a dish for all who are in a hurry, who like macaroni and who don't mind the calories. Get very thick macaroni of the seashell variety. Boil it for about 12 minutes in salted water. Take out and drain well. Butter a baking pan, and put in it alternately a thin layer of macaroni, then a thick layer of grated cheese mixed with chopped parsley and beaten egg. When you have used up all the macaroni, put lots more cheese on top, sprinkle with paprika, and bake in a hot oven for 15 minutes. If you are making this dish for more than 4 people, use 2 beaten eggs.

Fowl

TURKEY

In Turkey, the American turkey is known as the Hindi, which means Indian or American bird.

If anyone is in search of a typical American dish, it isn't hamburger, it isn't doughnuts, and it isn't ham and eggs. The national dish is roast turkey.

The Pilgrims were the first American settlers to discover the wild turkey, ancestor of the present domestic bird. Anyone who has been exceedingly hungry, and has tasted wild turkey meat roasted over an outdoor fire, will understand why the Pilgrims were so fond of it. What interests me is the fact that this bird has been likened to the Turks because of the red feathers of the puskul, which is like the tassel the Turks used to wear on their fezzes. However, I still think it is the grandest bird to be served at a ceremonial dinner.

My twenty years of turkey cooking in this country, averaging about 50,000 pounds of bird a year, has taught me a new and unorthodox way of preparing it. It has become the chief delight of many lusty eaters who have visited my restaurants or whom I have served at outstanding functions in Hollywood and San Francisco.

I have found a way to keep turkey meat moist—yet it will have a crisp skin. When you cut it with a knife you will see the juices just oozing out of it. I use Armenian pilaff for the dressing. This, in my opinion, is better than any wild rice or bread stuffing. Of course, that is a matter of taste.

12- to 14-pound turkey
2 cupfuls tomato juice
1 cupful sherry
1 tablespoon paprika
2 tablespoonfuls salt
½ teaspoonful black pepper
2 whole carrots cut lengthwise
4 branches celery
6 cups water

After singeing and cleaning the turkey, put it in a roasting pan. Place carrots and celery inside the bird. Mix all other ingredients together and pour over the turkey. Add 6 cups of water. Bake in oven at 375 degrees for 3 hours, turning bird over every 30 minutes—that is, 4 times. Before the last half hour, remove turkey from oven. Take out celery and carrots, and stuff turkey with rice or bulghour pilaff dressing. Ten minutes before turkey is done, pour off all juices from roasting pan, and let the bird roast dry to complete browning.

RICE PILAFF DRESSING

½ pound butter
6 cupfuls long grain rice
1 cupful pine nuts (¼ pound)
1 cupful finely chopped onions
1 cupful currants or seedless raisins
⅔ teaspoonful cinnamon
⅔ teaspoonful allspice
1 teaspoonful black pepper
2 tablespoonfuls salt
all of cooked diced giblets, liver, and heart
12 cupfuls of broth

Melt butter in cooking pot, add rice, and braise for at least 10 minutes. Combine with pine nuts, currants, chopped onions, and the giblets which have been partly boiled in the broth pot. Add seasonings. Mix well, cover, and bake in oven for 30 minutes. Take out, mix well, and bake covered for another 20 minutes. This should be served under slices of turkey with gravy on top.

NOTE: Do not wash rice.

TURKEY GRAVY

Skin off surface fat from natural gravy which you have previously poured into a tall container. Place fat in skillet and gradually add 2 cupfuls of flour. Brown well and add ⅔ teaspoonful of allspice. Add natural gravy with enough hot water to obtain desired thickness. Cook at least 15 minutes. Salt to taste. Just before serving, strain the gravy. If you like a little more coloring, add paprika and tomato sauce.

TURKEY BROTH

Save and boil fat, neck, giblet, heart, and liver in 3 quarts water. Later giblet, liver, and heart should be used in pilaff dressing.

TURKEY WINGS

I have found a way to use turkey wings that appeals to many people. Cut off the wings from uncooked turkeys and boil them. When they are tender, remove the broth and make a rice pilaff. Then roll the wings in flour, fry in butter until tender and golden brown. Serve with pilaff and gravy.

TURKEY À LA KING

The best way to serve leftover turkey is à la king. If properly prepared, it is wonderful. Creamed turkey should usually be eaten at home, because there you will not be troubled with doubts about what you are eating. The secret of its success is in the way the sauce is made.

½ cube or ⅛ pound butter
¾ cupful flour
2 cupfuls milk
1 cupful turkey broth
salt and pepper

Brown flour in butter until light brown; that gives a nutty flavor which adds so much to your turkey. Then add liquids, stirring constantly to make a smooth sauce of the desired consistency.

CHICKEN TCHAKHOKHBELLI

This delicacy is to Georgians what turkey is to Americans. By Georgians, I mean people from the country of Georgia in the Caucasus; that Armenian neighbor has given to the world— and the movie colony—many outstanding head waiters and princes. It has been doubted sometimes whether the latter are really princes. Well, I can vouch for the fact that they really were princes before they came to this country, because to be a prince in Georgia is not as difficult as owning a hamburger stand in America. All you have to do is become the owner of two cows, one horse, and a plow, and you are a *gazovni*! Most famous of the Georgian princes here are the Mdivanis, and I have named my Tchakhokhbelli dish after them because it is their favorite dish, and has been ordered by all who have known them and then visited my restaurant.

I think Tchakhokhbelli is one of the best ways of cooking chicken. In fact, it is one of the few ways that actually does justice to that delicate bird. I want to call attention to the fact that I use a great deal of sherry in cooking fowl, for they have a natural affinity. Fowl differs from the average meat in that it tends to take on other flavors. Wine brings out the natural flavor of the bird.

    2 2-pound chickens (8 pieces)
    ¼ pound butter
    1 large onion sliced
    ½ cupful sherry
    ½ cupful tomato juice
    1 teaspoonful paprika
    1 teaspoonful salt
    pepper to taste

Melt butter in frying pan. Add chicken and braise until light brown. Remove chicken, and place in baking pan. Sauté onion in butter left in frying pan. Then add all other ingredients—wine, tomato juice, paprika, salt, pepper, 1 cup water—and pour over chicken in baking dish. Bake in oven at 400 degrees, without cover. Turn over after half hour. Cook for another half hour, then turn again and cook for 15 minutes. Serve with rice pilaff.

ROAST CHICKEN

    1 3½-pound roaster
    1 tablespoonful butter
    salt and pepper
    1 cupful water
    ½ teaspoonful paprika
    1 branch celery
    1 carrot

Clean chicken well, and stuff with celery and carrot. Baste with melted butter and seasonings. Add water and paprika. Roast in oven at 375 degrees for 2 hours, turning over every half hour. Serve with pilaff.

CHICKEN ARARAT

2 2½-pound fryers
1 glass sherry
½ pound fresh mushrooms
1 cupful chopped onions
2 cupfuls milk or cream
½ pound butter or 1 cupful
3 tablespoonfuls flour
2 cupfuls chicken soup stock
salt and pepper

Cut each chicken into 8 pieces. Fry in one-half of the butter and place in baking pan. Add sherry, salt, and pepper. Sauté onions and mushrooms in the same butter, and simmer until tender. Pour over chicken, add chicken stock, and simmer. Brown flour in rest of butter, adding cream or milk to make a smooth sauce. Pour this over the chicken when serving it, and sprinkle generously with chopped parsley.

CHICKEN SOUTHERN STYLE

2 2-pound fryers
salt and pepper
flour to dredge
butter or peanut oil
2 cupfuls milk

Soak cleaned and cut-up fryers in milk for at least 2 hours. Drain, salt and pepper the chicken, and roll in flour. Fry in a deep pan in butter or peanut oil until golden brown. Cover the pan and simmer for 20 minutes more. Take out chicken, and keep hot while making the following sauce.

LOUISIANA SAUCE

2 tablespoonfuls butter
1 tablespoonful flour
1 cupful soup stock
1 cupful milk
6 stoned and chopped ripe olives
½ cupful chopped mushrooms
3 tablespoonfuls sherry
salt and pepper

Brown flour in butter. Slowly add stock and milk. Cook to a smooth sauce. Add mushrooms, olives, and sherry. Serve with Chicken Southern Style, along with hot biscuits and honey, and shoestring potatoes.

CHICKEN FRICASSEE

1 4-pound tender hen
1 small onion
1 stalk celery
2 quarts of water
1 cube butter
½ cupful flour

Disjoint chicken and wash well. Boil hen with onion, celery, giblets, and salt and pepper. Remove from broth when chicken is tender and strain the broth. Brown flour in butter, and slowly stir in one-half of strained broth. Cook well. While this is simmering, cook noodles in other half of broth. Serve chicken, noodles, and sauce topped with chopped parsley and cooked green peas.

HERRISSAH
Armenian Traditional Chicken

3 cupfuls pearl barley, bulghour, or coarse wheat cereal

1 rooster (5 pounds)

1 gallon water

1 cube butter

salt and pepper

3 hours of elbow grease

Soak wheat overnight. Boil rooster with salt and pepper until very well done. Take out of broth, cool, bone and shred. Now put meat back into the broth into which you have poured the soaked barley or wheat. Cook until the barley soaks up all the broth. Then start beating with a wooden spoon. After a long, long beating, when you are all worn out, it should look like well-cooked oatmeal mush. Serve it in bowls, with a spoonful of browned butter poured into a depression in the middle of it. You will find it is well worth all the effort.

MUD HEN
Black Leghorns

It is not necessary to feather or skin a mud hen. With a sharp knife split breast; take out whole breast and legs. The breasts and legs are the only parts that are used.

Season bird with sherry and onions. Let it stay in refrigerator overnight. Brown in butter or oil, fry onions. Put hens and onions in a roasting pan, add a little tomato sauce, salt and pepper, and sherry and a little water. Bake in hot oven for 45 minutes, turning pieces every 15 minutes. Serve with wild rice.

ROAST GOOSE WITH SAUERKRAUT

1 goose of about 12 pounds

1 cupful tomato sauce or juice

⅔ cupful sherry

4 sprigs of celery

1 large cut carrot

3 cupfuls water

3 tablespoonfuls salt

½ teaspoonful pepper

1 tablespoonful goose fat

1 large onion

2 pounds sauerkraut

12 teaspoonfuls caraway seeds

1 large potato

½ cup of water

Put carrot and celery into the bird. Fry onion in fat, add sauerkraut and grated potato. Then add caraway seeds, salt, pepper, and water. Turn bird over every half hour. After 1½ hours, take out of oven. Take away carrots and celery and stuff it with sauerkraut and potato stuffing. Let it roast for another hour, dry, without any juice.

WILD DUCK or GOOSE

One cook's advice about wild fowl is: "De less you meddles wid 'em, de better dey be."

No sauces or strong flavors should be added to modify the flavor except where ducks thrive on fish and have a very strong fishy flavor. In that event, insert 1 carrot and a celery stalk in the carcass during baking process, and remove later.

No fowl should be cooked when taken direct from refrigerator. It should stand for a couple of hours in a warm place.

Sprinkle the duck or goose with sherry and then see that it is well larded or oiled with olive oil or peanut oil, or better yet 3 to 4 slices of fat bacon or salt pork put on breast.

It should be set in a very hot oven and basted every 4 minutes. Just before removing it, sprinkle lightly with salt and pepper. Fifteen to 20 minutes is ample time for rare duck; 30 to 40 minutes will have it thoroughly cooked.

Wild rice is a sportsman's favorite companion dish. Here is my simple and favorite rice recipe to go with the duck.

Take ¼ pound of butter. Melt in a pot, add 3 cups long grain rice, braise for 5 minutes, add 6 cups of broth (chicken, lamb, or beef); if you have no broth, use plain hot water. Add 2 teaspoonfuls salt, a little white pepper, and mix well. Cover pot and bake at 400 degrees for 40 minutes. Take out of oven, mix well, and bake for 10 more minutes.

Pilaff

PILAFFS are to Armenians and Near Easterners what potatoes are to Americans. Americans serve mashed potatoes, fried potatoes, baked potatoes, and so on. Armenians serve pilaffs, and the more ways you know to prepare pilaff, the better cook you are.

One would think that, since rice is a product of China, India, and the Indian and Pacific Ocean regions, the peoples of this area would have developed as many ways of preparing rice as have the Armenians. But they habitually serve boiled rice. Perhaps the reason is that they have used rice as their one basic food, like bread and meat, whereas we have tried to make it an exotic touch to meat, fowl, and vegetable courses. Pilaff is the essence of a fine dinner. How well I have found that out in the score of years I have served the American public. I have served thousands of different dishes, but invariably my patrons remember and ask for the pilaff—and especially the wheat pilaff.

We have again the old argument about the chicken and the egg, when we discuss whether rice or bulghour (wheat) pilaff came first. Since the Near East and the Caucasus are wheat-producing countries, and according to history and legend had long prepared wheat dishes before rice was introduced through the Persian influence, I believe that wheat was the original pilaff. Be that as it may, both are delectable.

I have found that the simplest way to prepare a good pilaff is to see that the grains are well braised in butter, and then the right amount of good broth added. I emphasize the broth be cause it is this good soup stock that makes the pilaff tasty. But if you do not have good broth, go a little heavy on the butter, then add plain water.

Do not use any vegetables or seasoning in making broth for pilaff, for this dish requires the plain flavor of chicken, veal, lamb, or beef.

The average rice bought in America for household use will absorb 2 cups of broth to 1 cup of rice. So, although different kinds of rice vary in this respect, this may be used as a basic measurement. Bake pilaff in an oven at about 375 degrees; this insures an even cooking of all the grains, and it seals in all the flavor.

In the following recipes those who like to experiment and who have the patience required for preparing special dishes will find several variations for cooking pilaffs.

BULGHOUR PILAFF

As far back as is known of the history of old countries like Armenia, Syria, Assyria, and Greece, the records show that wheat was the staple food. The first cultivation of wheat is credited to the Hittites, who were the forefathers of most Near Eastern peoples of today. That includes all of the Armenians, most of the Balkan people, all Caucasians, Syrians, Arabs, and Jews. The fighting peoples, like the Armenians, who migrated from the north of the Balkan peninsula, recognized the truly great agricultural genius of the Hittites and continued to develop in this field.

But we don't have to go back to history to learn that the processing of wheat, or bulghour, was discovered by accident. That's true of the discovery of many good foods, such as cookies, roast pork, and other things. The processing of wheat into bulghour was developed as a method of preserving it. I say "processing" because the bulghour retains its wheat flavor even after it has been treated in the following manner.

Whole kernels of wheat are boiled outdoors in huge cauldrons. Then the wheat is dried thoroughly in the sun. It must be done in weather that is so hot that the wheat will dry in one day, for if it remains in the open overnight it will mildew. The ancients didn't know why this processing of the wheat preserved it, but it has only recently been discovered by scientists that certain elements in the sun's rays actually preserve wheat and other cereals. Wheat is the only cereal that is absolutely resistant to bugs or mold when kept for three or more years.

Through this process, Armenians have developed a healthful and delicious food that has served the needs of all the hordes who have passed through the Balkan countries. Every conqueror in history has gone through there, and the land has been ravaged with famine and pestilence. Yet these peoples have been able to survive because they have been able to save, or somehow acquire, this bulghour which has given them enough vitamins to resist the effects of famine. It is a poor man's food, a staple.

You can get bulghour at any Armenian or Greek store. Cook it as follows:

3 cupfuls bulghour

1 cube (¼ pound) butter

1 small onion chopped fine

6 cupfuls broth—chicken, lamb, or beef

salt and pepper

Melt butter in heavy skillet, add dry bulghour. Braise well until butter begins to bubble. Fry onion in separate pan until golden brown. Mix with bulghour, and add broth and seasonings. Stir well, and bake in oven (375 to 400 degrees) for 30 minutes. Remove from oven, stir well, and bake again for 10 minutes.

RICE PILAFF

Rice pilaff is made in exactly the same way, and with the same proportions of ingredients, except that onions are omitted.

DOMATESLI PILAFF or PINK PILAFF
Pilaff with Tomato Juice or Paste

3 cupfuls rice

¼ pound butter

3 cupfuls tomato juice

3 cupfuls broth—chicken, lamb, or beef

salt and pepper

Melt butter in heavy frying pan. Add dry rice. Braise well until butter bubbles. Mix broth and tomato juice together and boil. Pour boiling mixed broth over rice. Add salt and pepper and mix well. Bake in oven (375 degrees) for 30 minutes. Take out, mix well again, and bake for 20 minutes more.

AJEM PILAFF
Persian Pilaff

1 pound shoulder of lamb

⅔ cupful chopped onion

½ cupful chopped fresh tomatoes, or

½ cupful solid-pack canned tomatoes

½ cube butter

2 cupfuls rice

broth or water

salt and pepper

Have butcher cut shoulder of lamb into 1-inch cubes. Braise well in pot. Add chopped onions and brown lightly with the meat. Add tomatoes and cook for 15 minutes.

Meanwhile soak 2 cups rice in heavily salted hot water. (This removes starch from rice.) Wash well in cold water, and put rice carefully over top of meat in the pot. In center of rice place the cube of butter. Pour 1 cupful water around the edges of the meat and bake in a moderate oven for 1 hour. Turn onto platter and serve unmixed and very hot.

Meats

Lᴀᴍʙ is the staple meat of the Near East. There are more ways of preparing it than any other kind of meat. I say this as an authority, not because I know more ways to cook lamb than any other cook in the world, but because I have traveled all over this globe and seen it done. It is unfortunate that in America we know so little about lamb. The fault does not lie with the housewife or average restaurateur, but with the growers and the butchers who have failed to educate consumers in ways to use all cuts of the animal.

There is, as you know, a great deal of difference between lamb and mutton. In the past, we have had no way of preventing the butcher or the restaurateur from selling mutton when lamb is requested. Hence a prejudice has arisen against it.

Lamb is the traditional ceremonial food in Armenia, as turkey is in America. Armenians roast lamb on their memorial days, or *Madagh*. People go to the churchyards for prayer, then afterwards they give the poor and needy a wonderful feast of roast lamb with pilaff.

I remember my first impression of the mountain folk in the Caucasus at the time when I marched over the rocky roads to get to Karabagh. In this remote country they have no inns such as you find in the lower plateaus. You automatically become the guest of the *melik*, or *keghia*, who is the mayor, the judge, the chief of police, and host par excellence. When you enter his home the daughter of the household, or the wife, brings a basin of water and you wash your feet. There could be no greater courtesy, for you have marched over sharp stones and rough vegetation, and probably your feet are sore and bleeding. Then you are presented with a brand new pair of woolen socks woven by members of the household from wool spun by the women-folk. They take away your soiled socks, and when you are ready to leave you find them with your belongings, mended and clean.

If you are a person of consequence, you become the guest of the whole village. You stand at evening in front of the *melik's* house, and everybody comes by to shake hands with you. At sundown you hear the bells of the flocks of sheep coming in. As they pass, the *melik* and some of the elders pick out the best horned ram in the flock, and the sheep-herder drives the rest of the flock home.

Then he returns and starts carving the ram, which has been slaughtered. Through my profession and travels I have seen many master butchers and chefs who know how to handle a knife. But never have I seen anything like the skill of a shepherd of the Caucasian mountains when it comes to skinning a lamb from an opening in the neck of not more than 6 or 8 inches. With a single sharp-edged knife, he slits the skin of the animal, then pulls the body of the lamb from that little opening. He then removes the intestines, takes the lamb to the spring, and washes it thoroughly. He stuffs the cavity with pilaff dressing, sews it up, seasons it well, and then puts it back into the skin.

The lamb is then placed in a prepared pit. It is about 5 feet deep, and leaves are placed in the bottom. The lamb is covered with about 4 inches of dirt, so that the fire doesn't touch the skin. Then burning logs are put over it—enough to burn most of the night—and while this is flaming and sparkling the villagers make merry. Everybody turns out, including musicians and *ashoughs,* who are like our minstrels.

But the day of all days is the following one. The lamb is taken out of the pit and put on a huge table. The priest of the village blesses it. The man who is to carve the lamb waits until everybody holds a candle that has been made from beeswax by the priest himself. Our host, the *melik,* takes a light from the priest and carries it over to the guest of honor, who is the only person in the congregation who has a right to light more than one candle. The guest then lights the candle of his neighbor to the right and left, and so it is passed around. Not until then is the lamb carved. I challenge anyone who has partaken of this to name a dish that tastes more delicious.

When the skin is removed from the roasted lamb you see the juiciest meat imaginable. But the juice disappears rapidly, because everybody has provided himself with a hunk of bread and is ready to reach over and dunk in it. Then he waits for his pilaff and piece of meat. And here one custom, originating long before Christ, still exists. You eat with your hands, for the use of knives and forks is taboo.

SHISH KEBAB

Naturally a whole roast lamb cannot be served on every ceremonial occasion. So shish kebab or khorovadz has been evolved. This is to Armenians what corned beef and cabbage is to the Irish. It is like the Russian shashlik.

The history of shashlik dates far back, but the known origin can be traced to the mountain folk of the Caucasus who, during their migrations, would kill wild game, stick it on their swords, and roast it over the fire. Hence the name shish kebab, which means barbecue or skewer, for which the sword served.

All during the years we have served shish kebab, this has been one of our most popular dishes. It is made of lamb seasoned in sherry, onion, and orégano, an herb that grows in all the Mediterranean countries. The combination of these three gives a flavor similar to garlic but with none of the aftertaste. Always serve shish kebab with pilaff. To make shish kebab use:

1 leg of lamb (5 or 6 pounds)
½ pound onions
1 tablespoonful salt
½ teaspoonful pepper
⅓ cup sherry
2 tablespoonfuls oil
1 teaspoonful orégano

Remove all fat and gristle from the leg of lamb. Bone it and cut into 1-inch squares. Mix meat with sliced onions, seasonings, and other ingredients. Let meat marinate in sauce at least an hour, and preferably overnight. Put on skewers and broil over charcoal fire or gas broiler until crisply brown on all sides.

BAKED LAMB CHOPS

8 thick loin chops
2 large tomatoes, quartered
2 large onions, sliced
2 cupfuls water
⅓ cupful parsley
½ teaspoonful paprika
1 tablespoonful salt
pepper to taste
1 teaspoonful orégano

Set chops in open baking pan. Add onions, parsley, tomatoes, salt, pepper, paprika, and water. Bake in oven for 45 minutes. Remove from oven, turn chops over, and bake for another 30 minutes.

BAKED SHOULDER OF LAMB
WITH VEGETABLES

3 pounds shoulder of lamb, with blade bone
1 pound potatoes
1 pound carrots
1 large can tomatoes
¼ pound turnips
salt and pepper
3 cupfuls water

Wash lamb well. Place in roasting pan. Around it arrange diced vegetables. Add tomatoes, seasonings, and water. Cover and bake in hot oven for about 1½ hours. Take off cover and bake for an additional 20 minutes, or until nicely browned.

BAKED BREAST OF LAMB

2 pounds breast of lamb
salt and pepper

Wash lamb well. Bake in open pan with salt and pepper for 2 hours. Have oven at 375 degrees; turn over three times, or every half hour to brown evenly on all sides. Serve with rice pilaff.

KOUZOU KZARTMA
Roast Shank of Lamb

4 shanks of lamb
4 large pieces of potato
2 tomatoes, quartered

2 teaspoonfuls salt
1 teaspoonful paprika
2 cupfuls water

Wash lamb well and let it stand in clean water for at least

15 minutes. Place in open roasting pan; add tomatoes, salt, paprika, and water. Cook for half an hour at 375 degrees, turn meat over and cook for another half hour. Now add potatoes to same pan and roast with the shanks for 30 minutes, then turn both potatoes and meat and let cook for another 30 minutes. Meat should cook for 2 hours all together. Serve with its own juice as gravy.

AMERICAN MEAT LOAF À LA MARDIKIAN

2 pounds meat (lamb, beef, or veal, either fresh or cooked)

2 large chopped onions

2 large bell peppers chopped

½ cupful finely chopped parsley

1 cupful breadcrumbs or 6 slices of dry bread

2 raw eggs

½ teaspoonful allspice or camino

½ teaspoonful powdered mustard

½ cupful tomato juice

salt and pepper to taste

4 hardboiled eggs for stuffing

Put meat, peppers, onions, and parsley through the meat grinder. Mix all together in a large mixing bowl; add bread, and all other ingredients. Break in the 2 raw eggs and combine thoroughly. Form into a roll, putting hardboiled eggs in the center of the meat. Roll it in greased patapar paper, making a package with both ends sealed. Put in baking dish and bake for 1½ or 2 hours in moderate oven. Delicious served hot or cold.

HAGGIS

Several times I have served what I call a Scottish Feast in my restaurants. It is always very popular, and recipes and menus are much in demand. The menu for the dinner is this:

Scotch Barley Broth
Haggis
Scottish Biscuits
Kippered Herring with boiled potatoes
Combination Vegetable Salad, using no tomatoes or asparagus
Finnan Haddie (haddock)
Roast Beef, well done, with natural gravy and mashed turnips
and boiled kale
Plum Pudding

That is not a meal one can contemplate serving every day. But try this recipe for haggis.

2 lamb tripes; soak overnight in cold water

lamb's liver, heart, and lungs; soak this overnight also

½ pound suet of beef

1 pound oatmeal

1 pound onions

4 tablespoons salt

½ teaspoonful pepper

Grind the lamb liver, heart, lungs, and the suet of beef, and mix well with all the other ingredients. Stuff this mixture into the tripe. With a big needle sew up the openings, making a bag of the tripe. Place a couple of plates upside down on the bottom of a large kettle. Put the haggis on top of these, cover with water, and cook with lid on kettle for 5 hours over a slow fire. Serve on a large platter. The head of the household should slice with a knife and serve to guests.

BEEF À LA STROGANOFF

2 pounds lean beef, sliced ¼ inch thick, and cut into
   2-inch strips
1 cupful chopped onions
1 cupful mushrooms
½ cupful tomato juice
1 pint water or beef stock
½ cupful sherry
1 cube butter or ½ cupful
salt and pepper for seasoning
sour cream (smetana)

Dip strips of beef in flour. Fry in butter for 5 minutes. Remove and place in baking dish. Fry onions in same butter until slightly cooked. Pour them over the meat, adding mushrooms, tomato juice, wine and stock, and seasonings. Bake in oven (375 degrees) for 30 minutes. Serve on piece of toast, with sour cream on top.

ARMENIAN BAKED STEAK

2 pounds rump steak, ½ inch thick (cut in 6 pieces)
   pounded
1 large onion chopped fine
1 large bell pepper chopped
½ cupful chopped celery
½ cupful sherry
½ teaspoonful paprika
½ cupful tomato sauce or juice
1 cupful water
salt and pepper to taste

Season steak with salt and pepper. Dip in flour and fry in butter or oil for 1 minute on each side. Place in pan suitable for baking. In frying pan sauté chopped onion, pepper, and celery. Add wine, tomato sauce, paprika, and water. Bake uncovered in oven at 375 degrees for 30 minutes. Turn steaks over and bake for another 30 minutes.

ROAST VEAL WITH SAGE DRESSING

2- to 3-pound veal roast, either shoulder or leg
   (have butcher bone and roll it)
1 onion
1 chopped carrot
1 cupful tomato juice
salt and pepper

Place roast in open roasting pan. Add vegetables, juice, and seasonings. Bake for 3 hours in moderate oven. Do not baste, but turn roast over every half hour after first hour. Slice and serve with gravy on top of dressing.

To make gravy: Brown 4 tablespoonfuls flour in 2 tablespoonfuls butter. Add juice from roasting pan, and more water or broth if required. If desired, add 1 tablespoonful allspice while gravy is cooking.

DRESSING:

½ loaf bread
1 large sliced onion
1 teaspoonful sage
salt and pepper
2 tablespoonfuls butter
bouillon or broth

Slice and toast bread and cut up into 1-inch pieces. Pour hot bouillon or broth over it. When it is well soaked, add onion that has been sautéed in butter. Put in sage, salt, and pepper, and mix well. Pile lightly in open buttered pan; sprinkle paprika over the top and bake in oven with roast for at least ½ hour. To add flavor and body to this dressing, 2 raw eggs may be broken into it as it is being mixed.

STUFFED PORK CHOPS

rib chops—cut in pairs, with a pocket between
1 large onion chopped and sautéd in ⅓ cupful peanut
     oil or butter
¼ cupful parsley
¼ cupful raw rice
allspice and cinnamon to taste
salt and pepper
½ cupful water

Cook together all ingredients except chops, and simmer gently for ½ hour. Then stuff into pocket cut between the chops. Place side by side in baking pan and bake until brown. Then turn over and brown other side. For quicker cooking, chops may be stuffed and partly fried before baking.

BAKED HAM À LA OMAR

6 to 8 pounds corned pork (have butcher skin, bone,
     and roll it)
6 ounces brown sugar
6 slices of pineapple
whole cloves

Boil pork in large pot for 45 minutes; change water and boil for 45 minutes more. Let pork cool in cooking water, then remove and place in open baking pan. Sprinkle brown sugar all over it; place pineapple slices on top, and tack cloves all over meat. Pour the pineapple juice over it and bake in a moderate oven for 1 hour, basting every 15 minutes. When serving, place a red cherry in the center of pineapple slices, and serve with sweet potatoes.

To make gravy: Brown ½ cupful flour in butter and stir in all juices from the baking pan. Add water to make proper consistency, and cook well. Put through a sieve, and add boiled raisins and cubed pineapple. Serve over sliced ham.

KUFTÉ

Like a kid saving the biggest bite till the last, we have saved our favorite meat recipes until the end of the chapter.

Kuftés are used in Armenia for basic quick dinners. All are made with ground meats, the most popular one being Izmir Kufté, which means meat ball of Smyrna. It is a glorified hamburger, given a nice Near Eastern touch by the addition of cummin (spice), and a good bit of parsley and onion. Kuftés can be made with any kind of ground meat, or a mixture of several kinds.

IZMIR KUFTÉ

1 pound ground meat
1 raw egg
½ cupful finely chopped onion
¼ cupful very finely chopped parsley
1 cupful soaked bread or toasted crumbs
½ teaspoonful cummin
salt and pepper

Mix all ingredients together, and form into thumb-shaped patties. Fry in butter if you are in a hurry, but they are more delicious if baked in a well-buttered pan in a very hot oven. Serve with pilaff.

BOLSAGAN KUFTÉ

This kufté is a favorite of folks around Istanbul. Its difference is that it is a hot, stew-like dish, with the kufté formed into round balls the size of a walnut. They are boiled in meat broth and just before serving the broth is thickened with a lemon-egg mixture. This is without doubt the most popular dish to be found in the Hellenic world.

    1 pound ground meat, preferably lamb shoulder
    ¼ cup parsley
    ½ cupful chopped onions
    ½ cupful uncooked rice
    3 eggs
    juice of 2 lemons
    2 tablespoonfuls flour
    salt and pepper
    ½ gallon meat broth

Mix well with the meat 1 raw egg, the vegetables, rice, and seasonings. Make into balls the size of walnuts. Roll in flour and gradually drop into boiling, seasoned broth. When all are in, cook until the rice is tender. Then beat the 2 remaining eggs with the lemon juice until very light and fluffy. Pour some broth over this mixture, whipping constantly to keep a creamy mixture. Return this to the broth and meat balls. Stir quickly and serve at once in deep soup bowls. For variation, use dried or chopped mint in this kufté if you like the flavor.

HARPUT KUFTÉ

This kufté is most popular in America—in fact, it is more popular here than in Armenia. The reason is that most of the Armenians in this country come from Harput, where the first American missionaries were established. Here was built the Euphrates American College, which had a great deal to do with starting the Armenian migration to America.

Harput kufté is a stuffed meat ball, and it may be served either with its broth or dry.

    1 pound ground lean beef or lamb
    1 cupful very fine bulghour (cracked wheat)
    salt and pepper

To prepare kufté, mix meat and cracked wheat with salt and pepper. Knead for 15 minutes till blended into a gummy mixture. Make into balls the size of a walnut by rolling in the palm of hand. With the thumb, make a hollow in each ball to hold the stuffing and press the side walls thin. Slip in stuffing and press top of ball closed, smoothing the place and sealing it by rolling ball between the palms. Stuffed balls are then dropped into boiling seasoned soup stock which has been cooking for 1 hour with ¼ cupful chopped parsley, ½ cupful onion, and 1 cup tomatoes. When the kuftés are cooked, they will rise to the surface. This will take about 20 minutes. Do not cook too many in the pot at one time, since they require room to rise.

Remove from soup stock. If kuftés are to be served dry, heat in butter in the oven to make a crisp crust. Or they may be served with soup stock in deep bowls. Try not to break the surface of the balls when removing them from soup stock, or you will lose some of the spicy juices that have been sealed inside.

See stuffing recipe on next page.

STUFFING:

1 large sliced onion

1 cube butter or ½ cupful

2 tablespoonfuls pine nuts

2 tablespoonfuls chopped parsley

¼ teaspoonful allspice

¼ teaspoonful ground cinnamon

2 tablespoonfuls currants (optional)

To prepare stuffing, fry onion in butter to the stage just before it turns pink, or, as Armenians say, until it is well killed. Add parsley and other ingredients and cook together for 5 minutes. Put in a dish and chill in refrigerator. When chilled, make into a ball the size of a large marble, and insert this into hollow of meat ball.

XIII

Meats Cooked with Vegetables

ONE of the major aims of this book is to teach Americans to cook vegetables in an entirely new fashion. I mean that I want them to get away from the habit of boiling vegetables, as they usually do, throwing away the juice—the best part—and then eating the "wood." So to me this is the most important chapter in the book.

My mother was partial to vegetables, and she was a typical, average Armenian housekeeper. The method I am now going to suggest, therefore, isn't my invention. It represents centuries of trial and error in bringing out the best in vegetables to please generations of gourmets.

By learning to make the following meat and vegetable combinations, I feel that you will be well repaid, for by cooking the two together, you not only improve the flavors of the foods but you retain all of the food values that are so often lost in cooking.

As I have mentioned before, this cuisine depends upon the food itself to give a fine flavor. It does not use condiments to season a fine piece of meat or a choice vegetable.

Armenians are very partial to baking foods instead of frying them. I have always claimed that one of the worst enemies of American health has been the frying pan. Proof? Take your frying pan and fry a couple of fresh tomatoes in butter. Then break in a couple of eggs (so that you won't waste the butter and tomatoes). This will make a good breakfast. But note the difference in the pan when you have taken the food out. The frying pan will be all shined up, but the tomatoes and eggs will have picked up all the flavors and discoloration from the pan.

These meat and vegetable recipes aim, by baking and proper cooking, to preserve every unit of all the vitamins, and so contribute to the health of the nation.

We will start off with a series of misovs; *misov* means with meat.

MISOV PAGLA
Fresh Fava or Horse Beans

1 pound shoulder of lamb, cut up for stew
1 cupful sliced onions
2 pounds tender, stringless fava beans
2 tablespoonfuls chopped fresh dill
salt and pepper
water

Braise meat until nicely browned; add onions and cook for 15 minutes. Cut up fava beans into lengths as you would string beans. Add dill seasoning, salt and pepper, and water to half cover. Put on lid and bake or steam until tender.

MISOV GANANCH LOBIA
String Bean Stew

1 pound shoulder of lamb, cut for stew
1 cupful sliced onions
2 pounds string beans
1 cupful fresh or canned tomatoes
salt and pepper
3 cupfuls water

Braise meat until brown; add onions and cook for 15 minutes. Cut string beans lengthwise and add to meat. Pour over tomatoes and water, salt and pepper, and bake covered until tender. Or you may steam this stew on top of the stove, if tightly covered.

MISOV SPANNAK
Spinach Stew

1 pound tender shoulder of lamb
1 cupful sliced onions
2 pounds cleaned spinach
1 cupful tomato juice or sauce
salt and pepper
1 cupful water

Braise meat until brown, add onions and cook slowly for 15 minutes so that onions will cook but not brown. Add spinach cut into large pieces, tomato juice, salt and pepper, and water. Cover and cook until well blended. This will take about 1 hour.

This is an exceptionally delicious combination, and is good for vitamin-conscious cooks. Be sure to dunk your bread in the juice of this stew in order to use every drop.

MISOV SISSAIR
Garbanzo or Chick-Pea Stew

1 pound shoulder of lamb, cut up
1 cupful sliced onions
1 pound garbanzos that have been soaked overnight
1 cupful tomato purée
salt and pepper
1 teaspoonful paprika
4 cupfuls water

Braise meat until brown; add onions and cook for 10 minutes. Add garbanzos and all other ingredients, and cook covered for 2 hours, or until chick-peas are thoroughly tender.

MISOV SEMPOOG
Eggplant Stew

1 pound shoulder of lamb, cut for stew
2 pounds eggplant
½ pound onions sliced (about 1 cupful)
½ pound fresh tomatoes, or 1 cupful canned
salt and pepper
1 teaspoonful paprika
3 cupfuls water

Braise meat until brown; add onions and braise with meat until soft. Cut eggplant into 2-inch cubes, and add to meat mixture. Pour over tomatoes, salt, pepper, paprika and water, and bake for 1 hour.

MISOV BAMIA
Okra with Meat

1 pound shoulder of lamb, cut for stew
1 large onion, sliced
1 pound okra
½ pound tomatoes cut up
1 whole lemon
salt and pepper
3 cupfuls water

Braise meat until brown; add onions and cook for 10 minutes. To prepare okra, remove stems without making an opening in the end of the pods. This will prevent the sticky juice from running out, and will make the stew more palatable. Add okra to meat mixture. Prick holes in a whole lemon with a fork, and drop this in with the okra. This will counteract the juices of the okra, to which some people object. Add also the tomatoes, salt, pepper, and water. Cook for 1 hour, tightly covered.

You may use young green grapes instead of the lemon for keeping the okra crisp and whole.

NOTE: Get medium-sized okra, and you will find it is more delicate in flavor.

MISOV DEREVAPATAT
Stuffed Grape Leaves

This is another truly Armenian dish that should become a favorite with cooks in all parts of the country where grape leaves are obtainable. If they cannot be found in your locality, substitute cabbage or lettuce leaves.

    1 pound ground shoulder of lamb
    ½ pound onions, chopped finely
    2 tablespoonfuls chopped parsley
    ¼ cupful rice
    1 teaspoonful salt
    black pepper to taste
    juice ½ lemon
    ⅓ cupful tomato purée

Boil grape leaves until half cooked. Mix well all other ingredients and roll up in grape leaves in small packages about 3 inches long by ¾ inch thick. Place in rows in a baking dish, and cover with water. Cover pan and bake in oven for 1 hour. Serve hot.

A delicious sauce is made by mixing madzoon with the gravy

in which the grape leaves are cooked. Pour this over the grape leaves, to make a delicious and different light luncheon dish.

MISOV PRASSA
Leek Stew

Leek is a vegetable relatively little used in this country, but it is very delicious, inexpensive, and nutritious when properly prepared. Try this combination:

    1 pound shoulder of lamb, cut for stew
    2 pounds leek
    1 can whole tomatoes
    salt and pepper
    4 cupfuls water

Braise meat until brown, and add tomatoes. Cut leeks into 2-inch lengths, discarding the outer, dark-green portion of the vegetable. Be sure that all silt is removed from between the stalks. Add to meat, together with seasonings and water. Cover tightly and cook over slow fire for 2 hours.

Armenians have a special bread for dunking, and you will find Armenian stews more juicy than most American varieties. If you prefer not to dunk, use less water.

MISOV KEREVIZ
Celery Root Stew

    1 pound shoulder of lamb, or beef for stew, cut in
       1-inch pieces
    2 pounds celery root, peeled and cut into 2-inch cubes
    1 large onion, sliced
    juice of 1 lemon
    2 eggs
    3 cupfuls water

Braise meat until lightly browned. Add onions and cook for 10 minutes. Put in celery root, salt, and pepper. Cover and cook for 1 hour or more, until celery root is tender. When done, beat the eggs well, and whip in the lemon juice, blending thoroughly. Take some of the hot liquid from the stew, and gradually add it to the egg-lemon mixture, beating all the time to keep the egg from curdling. When smooth, pour the mixture quickly into the stew. Mix and serve at once. This is an unusual dish, and is a very good way to prepare the little-used celery root.

TURLU GUVEJ
Combination Stew

This is probably the most frequently cooked dish in all the Balkans. It has everything.

1 pound shoulder of lamb, cut for stew

1 large sliced onion

1 large bell pepper, sliced

½ pound of tomatoes, diced

½ pound of string beans

½ pound eggplant, cut in 2-inch cubes

½ pound zucchini, cut in 1-inch cubes

¼ pound thinly sliced carrots

¼ pound okra (optional)

salt and pepper

paprika to taste

water to cover

Braise meat well; add onions and bell peppers and braise for 0 minutes more. Put this mixture in a roasting pan, and add other vegetables that have been mixed together. Salt, pepper, and sprinkle with paprika. Cover with water, then cover roaster tightly and bake in the oven at 375 degrees for 2 hours. The blended flavors are superb.

OLD-FASHIONED BEEF STEW

1 pound beef, cut for stew
1 large onion sliced
2 teaspoonfuls flour
1 pound potatoes, diced in 1-inch pieces
½ pound carrots, sliced
1 cupful tomatoes or purée
salt and pepper
1 bay leaf
1 teaspoonful paprika
water to cover

Braise beef until brown; add sliced onion and cook for 15 minutes. Then sprinkle flour lightly over meat and stir into juices. Brown lightly, then add tomatoes and bay leaf. Boil carrots and potatoes separately, and when almost done add to the stew, with their juices. Season with salt, pepper, and paprika. Add water to partly cover. Let simmer until blended and vegetables are tender but not mushy.

PATLIJAN KARNI YARIK
Stuffed Eggplant

2 eggplants
1 pound ground shoulder of lamb
1 large onion chopped
¼ cupful parsley
2 tomatoes
tomato sauce

Cut whole eggplants lengthwise into quarters. Salt generously and let stand for ½ hour. Slit each quarter in the middle, down to the rind, but do not break the outer skin. Fry the eggplant in butter until partly soft. Then stuff it with the braised meat, to which onions and parsley have been added, putting slices of tomato over the top. Put in baking pan; add water and tomato sauce and bake in oven for 40 minutes.

VICTORY GARDEN DOLMA
Stuffed Peppers, Zucchini, Tomatoes

1 pound ground shoulder of lamb
½ cupful rice
2 chopped onions (about ½ pound)
1 large chopped tomato, or half of small can of
   tomato sauce
3 teaspoonfuls chopped parsley
1½ teaspoonfuls salt
¼ teaspoonful pepper
fresh chopped mint or tarragon leaves, to add zest

Mix all ingredients together. Scoop out centers of good-size zucchinis that have been cut in 3-inch lengths. Remove seeds from bell peppers and hollow out tomatoes. Stuff filling into vegetables, and place in baking pan. Partly cover with water, and bake in oven for 1 hour. You do not need gravy, for the sauce itself will serve that purpose.

HAIGAGAN KEBAB
Armenian Mystery Package

This is one of the most popular and delicious of all the dishes that we serve in the Omar Khayyam restaurants, as well as one of the most nutritious.

2 pounds shoulder of lamb cut in 4 pieces

2 bell peppers cut in halves

2 tomatoes halved

1 onion cut in 4 pieces

1 eggplant cut in 4 pieces

1 large potato cut in 4 pieces

salt and pepper

patapar paper

Put in the center of each of 4 pieces of patapar paper 1 8-ounce piece of lamb, ½ pepper, ½ tomato, ¼ onion, ¼ eggplant, and ¼ potato. Salt and pepper each unit, and wrap it up in the patapar paper, making it into a compact package. Place side by side in a roasting pan, and bake in oven (375 degrees) for 3½ hours. Do not turn package or cover pan. Do not use water as there is enough moisture in the vegetables and meat to make a delicious natural gravy.

Leave in individual packages until served at the table. The aroma as the package is opened is delicious, and it is like a game to see what you are going to get to eat.

PATLIJAN À LA NAZ

10 slices eggplant, ¼ inch thick

1 pound lamb shoulder, ground

1 onion

⅓ cup parsley

salt and pepper

10 slices bacon

Salt slices of eggplant and let stand for ½ hour. When soft, wash in cold water. Mix together ground lamb, onion, parsley, salt, and pepper. Place 1 large spoonful of this mixture on each slice of eggplant. Roll up, wrap bacon around each roll, and fasten with toothpicks. Place in baking pan, and add 1 cup water and ½ cup tomato sauce. Bake for 1¼ hours, turning rolls over at the end of 45 minutes to brown both sides.

PATLIJAN HUNKAR
Eggplant Royal Style

In the few years I lived in Constantinople, the city burned to the ground four times. In each case they traced the origin of the fire to someone who was broiling patlijan over an open fire, so be careful when you broil eggplant.

    2 large eggplants
    1 pound lamb, cut into 1-inch squares
    1 small chopped onion
    2 tablespoonfuls tomato purée
    1 tablespoonful butter
    1 cupful water
    salt and pepper

Braise lamb in butter, and when brown add onions and sauté until golden in color. Add tomato purée, water, salt and pepper, and mix together. Cover pan and cook on top of stove or bake in the oven for about 1 hour. Meantime, make the second half of the dish as follows:

    2 tablespoonfuls flour
    2 tablespoonfuls butter
    1 cupful milk
    1 tablespoonful cheese, grated

Broil eggplant over open fire. Don't be alarmed when the skin gets black or burned. When eggplant is soft, drop it into cold water to make it easier to handle. Peel off the skin and mash the eggplant. Now melt butter in a saucepan and add flour. Brown lightly and gradually add milk and grated cheese to make a cream sauce. Add this to the mashed eggplant and beat well until the mixture is about the consistency of light, fluffy, mashed potatoes. Heat again in oven or in a steamer, and pile on a dinner plate with a ladleful of lamb sauté on top of each serving. Sprinkle fresh, chopped celery over the meat. This is a royal dish indeed!

SOLDATZKY BORSCH
Russian Soldier's Stew

2 pounds lean short ribs of beef

1 pound cabbage, cut in large pieces

½ pound potatoes, cubed

½ pound beets, sliced

¼ pound carrots, sliced

1 large onion, chopped

1 bunch parsley

1 whole lemon

4 tablespoonfuls sour cream (optional)

salt and pepper to taste

Cover short ribs of beef with water and boil with onion and parsley for 1 hour. Remove beef and strain juice. Throw away onions and parsley. Cook sliced beets and carrots in broth and then add potatoes and cabbage. Pierce the lemon with a fork, and drop whole into the stew. Cook covered until vegetables are done. Serve on large-platter with meat in center, surrounded by vegetables and broth. A dab of smetana (sour cream) should be put on top of each serving.

HAIGAGAN PILAFF

1 pound shoulder of lamb, cubed
1½ cupfuls of long grain rice
4½ cupfuls of water
salt and pepper

Season cubed lamb with salt and pepper. Pack into an enamel cup or small pan, and turn upside down in a baking dish or cooking pot. Place a weight on cup. Add 3 cups of water and cook slowly for about 1½ hours. Wash rice and put into pan around the cup. Add 1½ cupfuls water. Cover pan tightly, and bake for about 35 minutes, or until rice is done. Turn upside down on a large plate, and serve without mixing meat into rice, and without disturbing rice ring. Garnish with chopped parsley, and serve at once.

ARMENIAN SQUASH LOAF

2 pounds zucchini
1 pound ground lamb shoulder
1 cupful chopped onions
⅓ cupful chopped parsley
2 eggs
2 sliced tomatoes
1 cupful water
salt and pepper

Braise meat. Add onions and let cook for 10 minutes. Add beaten eggs, parsley, salt and pepper, and mix well. Slice zucchini lengthwise in strips ¼ inch thick. Place a layer of zucchini in bottom of baking dish. Add a layer of the meat mixture, and another of zucchini until all have been used up. Place layer of tomato over the top, and pour water over it. Bake for 1 hour in a moderate oven (375 degrees). Serve with rice pilaff.

ARTICHOKE ARMENIAN STYLE

6 large artichokes
½ pound ground shoulder of lamb
6 slices of tomato
2 medium-sized onions chopped
1 tablespoonful pine nuts
1 tablespoonful chopped parsley
¼ teaspoonful allspice
1 egg
2 cups water
juice of 1 lemon
salt and pepper

Cut off artichoke tops, leaving two-thirds of the heart and bottom. Scoop out inside leaves and all the fuzz. Braise meat with onions; add nuts, parsley, allspice, and pepper. When nicely braised, add raw egg to mixture to hold it together. Stuff this into center of artichokes. Place in a deep baking pan; add water and lemon juice. Cover each artichoke with a slice of tomato. Cover the pan, and bake in moderate oven for 1½ hours. Serve hot with its own juice poured over.

XIV

Vegetables

COOKING being both my vocation and avocation, I have studied foods that are not only palatable but beneficial. I have discovered that the people in the Near East know more about cooking vegetables than any other people. Perhaps one reason for this is that it is the center of the olive oil belt, and they have learned the secret of cooking vegetables with oil.

People living in Mediterranean countries use large quantities of olive oil, and for that reason not more than one person in a thousand is troubled with constipation. The oil keeps them in perfect condition.

A man will sit down with a whole loaf of bread, a handful of olives, and some wine. When he has finished eating, he will go out and do the work of a superman. There is another reason for his strength. Dried beans have more food value than any other vegetable. A person in Turkey, for instance, will boil a potful of beans with olive oil. Then he puts the pot on his head and goes to sections where men are working, and sells the beans to the workers. The worker carries a loaf of bread under his arm, and when he is ready to eat, he sits down on the ground cross-legged, takes off his turban, and places it in his lap. He then takes his bowl of beans, and with his knife cuts his loaf of bread. He dunks the bread in the beans, and eats his fill. When he has finished eating, he collects all the crumbs that have fallen into his turban, and puts them into his mouth. Not too sanitary, according to our standards, but it is against his religion to leave any crumbs on the floor or ground.

It is important, then, that we learn the method of cooking vegetables in olive or peanut oil. I have become very partial to the latter also, because it has no heavy odor or flavor and yet it contains a very high food value.

One of the staple vegetables of Armenia is eggplant, and I hope some day it will be a favorite in this country, too. It is so easily raised, so easily kept, and so easily cooked when you know how.

Our chief eggplant delicacy is a dish called Imam Bayeldi, which literally means "the priest fainted." According to the legend, a Mohammedan priest called Imam was very fond of eggplant cooked with meat. Imam's wife, being one of those ladies who liked to entertain, had entertained a little later than usual one afternoon. To her consternation, she realized she had forgotten all about going to the butcher shop before closing time. Being very much afraid of her husband's ire, she was in quite a predicament. But she collected her wits, found in the basement a lot of vegetables, and by substituting them for the meat she created the dish called Imam Bayeldi.

When her husband came home and sat down beside the low table, she set before him a dish with a heavenly aroma. Imam liked it so much that he ate portion after portion. In fact, he ate so much that he couldn't move, and just lay down right there. Some visitors came in and asked, "What has happened to Imam?"

"*Imam bayeldi,*" his wife answered. And so the dish was named.

I have often served this dish at gourmets' dinners, and I have never seen anyone who hasn't been enthusiastic about it. It is the favorite dish of Alfred Lunt and Lynn Fontanne. This is how you make it.

IMAM BAYELDI

2 large eggplants

1 pound onions, sliced

½ pound green peppers

½ cupful chopped parsley

1 cupful olive or peanut oil

1 pound tomatoes, or 1 No. 2 can solid pack tomatoes

Cut the 2 eggplants into quarters, 8 pieces altogether. Salt them, and let them stand until they start to perspire. Dark water will ooze out of the pieces. Meanwhile, prepare the stuffing:

Slice onion and peppers and sauté gently in the oil. Just about the time these are soft, add tomatoes, parsley, salt and pepper, and cook for 2 minutes.

Wash eggplant, make a slit down the center of each segment, and stuff with the cooked vegetable combination. Add 2 cups of water, and bake in the oven for 1 hour.

This dish may also be sliced and served cold as an appetizer or salad.

SEMPOOG ARKAYAGAN
Eggplant with Nuts

20 round slices of unpeeled eggplant

2 cupfuls bread soaked in water

1 cupful garlic oil

1 cupful ground walnuts or almonds

juice of 1 lemon

1 teaspoonful salt

½ teaspoonful pepper

Salt eggplant and let stand for ½ hour until it gets soft. Wash well in cold water. Dip in batter made of ½ cupful milk, 2 tablespoonfuls flour, and 1 beaten egg. Fry in oil until golden brown. Let cool. Spread each slice with the following mixture: Soak bread and squeeze out the water. Mix bread with garlic oil, lemon juice, salt and pepper. Beat this mixture until very smooth and the consistency of paste. Mix in chopped nuts. Spread on slices of eggplant and serve cold as an appetizer.

LENTIL SAUTÉ

2 cupfuls lentils
1 sliced onion
2 tablespoonfuls chopped parsley
½ cupful olive or peanut oil
5 cupfuls water
salt and pepper

Soak lentils in water overnight and pour off water. Fry onions in oil. Boil lentils in 5 cups of fresh water. Add onions, parsley, and seasoning, and cook slowly until lentils are tender.

This dish may be served cold, for when vegetables are cooked in oil they are delicious served either hot or cold. They do not have the flat taste of vegetables cooked in water only.

BEAN YAHNI
Lima Bean or Soy Bean Stew

½ cupful olive or peanut oil
½ pound sliced onions
2 cupfuls chopped parsley
½ cupful tomatoes
1 pound dry lima or soy beans
salt and pepper

Brown onions lightly in oil for 15 minutes. Add tomatoes and parsley. Wash and add beans that have been soaked overnight. Season and add water to cover. Put lid on pot and simmer on top of stove until beans are tender. Bean yahni may be served hot or cold.

POTATO PLAKI

½ cupful oil

1 cupful sliced onion

1 clove garlic, chopped very fine (optional)

1 cupful tomatoes

½ cupful parsley

2 pounds potatoes cut in ½-inch squares

salt and pepper

3 cupfuls water

Brown onions and garlic in oil. Add other ingredients, cover pot tightly and simmer for 45 minutes, or until potatoes are tender but not mushy. Serve in bowls.

EGYPTIAN STEW

This is an exceptionally good dish for meatless days. It is tasty, nourishing, simple to make, and is always popular because of the choice blending of flavors. Everywhere in Egypt this dish is served, in bazaars and business sections, from small booths similar to our hot dog stands, and it is the aroma wafting down the streets that lures the customers.

½ cupful oil

1 cupful sliced onions

2 cupfuls corn, cut fresh from the cob

2 cupfuls zucchini

1 cupful lima beans soaked overnight

½ cupful green peppers, sliced

½ cupful tomatoes

½ cupful chopped parsley

water

Brown onions and peppers lightly in the oil. Add the beans and corn and small amount of water and simmer for ½ hour. Then add zucchini, tomatoes, parsley, and seasonings. Cook all together very slowly for 45 minutes. In the Near East, this dish is made with quite a lot of juice and is served in stew bowls.

BEAN PLAKI

1 pound white dry beans

1 cupful diced potatoes

1 cupful diced carrots

1 cupful chopped onions

½ cupful chopped parsley

2 cupfuls tomatoes

½ cupful olive or peanut oil

2 cloves garlic chopped very fine

salt and pepper to taste

Soak beans overnight. Wash them and cook in fresh water. After cooking beans for 1 hour, add all other ingredients and cook for 1 hour more. Serve hot as a main dish in stew bowls, or serve cold as a salad on a lettuce leaf with a slice of lemon.

HAIGAGAN STRING BEANS
Armenian String Beans

½ cupful peanut oil
1 cupful finely sliced onions
1 cupful fresh or canned tomatoes
1 pound string beans cut lengthwise
salt and pepper
2 cupfuls water

Heat oil in pot; add sliced onions and sauté for 15 minutes. Add tomatoes and beans, salt, pepper, and water. Put on lid and simmer for about 1½ hours. Serve hot or cold. Beans cooked in this fashion are a perfect combination with cold meats.

HAIGAGAN PEAS
Armenian Peas

½ cupful peanut or olive oil
1 cupful sliced onions
1 cupful tomatoes, fresh or canned
4 cupfuls shelled peas
salt and pepper
2 cupfuls water

Heat oil in pot in which vegetables are to be cooked. Add onions and sauté for 15 minutes. Then add tomatoes, then peas, salt, pepper, and water. Cover and cook slowly for about 45 minutes, or until peas are done. These also may be served hot or cold.

In case you wish to use canned peas, be sure to cook onions and tomatoes with the water for 30 minutes before putting in the peas. Then simmer all together for 15 minutes.

SPINACH WITH RICE

This is another delicious and nutritious dish for meatless days.

½ cupful oil
1 cupful sliced onions
2 pounds spinach
1 cupful rice
salt and pepper

Braise onions for 15 minutes. Wash and cut up spinach into large pieces, using stems and all. Place on top of onions, and pour washed rice over the top. Add 2 cups water, salt and pepper; cover tightly and cook over a slow fire until rice is done. This will take about 45 minutes. Do not stir, but allow flavors to blend as the ingredients steam together.

LEEK SAUTÉ

½ cupful oil
1 cupful onion
2 pounds leeks
½ cupful finely sliced carrots
½ cupful tomatoes
salt and pepper

Cut leeks into 2-inch lengths, using only the white and light green portions. Discard the dark green ends, and be sure that all silt is removed from stalks.

Sauté onions 15 minutes in oil. Then add carrots, tomatoes, leeks, salt and pepper, and cover with water. Cover pan tightly and steam vegetables for 1½ hours. Leeks, little used in America, have a delightfully delicate flavor when carefully cooked, and are very plentiful in most parts of the world. Their virtues have long been recognized by the Chinese and most people of Europe.

VICTORY GARDEN MEAL
for Meatless Days

¼ pound parsnips or celery root

½ pound carrots

½ pound potatoes

1 cupful chopped parsley

2 cupfuls sliced onions

1 cupful peanut or olive oil

salt and pepper

bell peppers, eggplant, and tomatoes to stuff

2 cupfuls tomato purée or sauce

Sauté onions in oil for 15 minutes. Then add shredded carrots, parsnips, or celery root, and cook for 15 minutes. Add shredded potatoes, parsley, salt and pepper, and cook until partly done. Stuff this vegetable mixture into the peppers, tomatoes, or eggplants, or a combination of the three, and set in a baking pan. Pour the purée on top and bake for 30 minutes. If any are left over, they are equally tasty when served cold for luncheon the following day.

MUSHROOM PLAKI

½ cupful olive or peanut oil
1 pound mushrooms
1 pound sliced onions
1 cupful chopped parsley
1 small clove garlic

Braise sliced onions and finely chopped garlic in oil and add parsley. Divide this mixture into two parts, and put one half into the bottom of a baking dish. Set whole mushrooms on top of mixture and cover with second half of onion mixture. Add 1 cup of water, salt and pepper, and bake covered for 45 minutes. Serve with slices of lemon for an unusual luncheon dish, or as a vegetable with dinner.

FRITTERS
Banana, Pineapple, Apple, etc.

2 eggs
1 pint milk
½ cupful sugar
2 tablespoonfuls baking powder
3 cupfuls flour
1 tablespoonful oil
1 teaspoonful vanilla extract

Beat eggs, add sugar, milk, and oil, and stir well. Sift flour and baking powder together. Add to egg mixture and beat until smooth.

Fill frying pan half full of peanut oil, or frying fat, and heat until very hot. Dip fruit into batter and drop into hot fat. Fry until golden brown. Remove carefully so as not to break crust, and drain on brown paper or paper towel. Serve plain as a vegetable, or with whipped cream sprinkled with your favorite seasoning for dessert. Or make a sauce from fruit juices.

NOHOUD KUFTÉ
Garbanzo Cutlets

1 cupful mashed potatoes
2 egg yolks
1 pound garbanzo beans soaked overnight
½ cupful finely chopped onions
¼ cupful finely chopped parsley
salt and pepper
oil to fry in

Cook beans for an hour. Put through a sieve to remove skins, and mix in beaten egg yolks, chopped onion, potatoes, parsley, salt and pepper. When thoroughly mixed, make into small walnut-sized balls. Fry these in deep oil and serve hot for the main dish on meatless days.

PEAS AND CARROTS BASDI

1 pound sliced carrots
½ cupful olive or peanut oil
1 cupful finely sliced onion
½ cupful tomatoes, fresh or canned
1 No. 2 can of peas
salt and pepper
1 cupful water

Brown onions in oil; add sliced carrots and tomatoes. When carrots are almost done, put in peas and simmer together for 15 minutes. This may be served hot or cold.

XV

Desserts

IF YOU want to eat like a true Armenian, your desserts will be comprised of little besides fruits. Fresh fruits when they are in season, and in the wintertime compotes made of stewed prunes, apricots, pears, raisins (both seedless and muscat), and every imaginable dried fruit. Stew them separately or put them all together and cook them into a compote. That will be your every-day dessert.

But when Armenians have a special function, they use their culinary skill to create exotic desserts—fifty-six-layer pastry, all sorts of cakes, anooshbadar, which means "the sweet bite," khadayiff with kaymuk, and many puddings, including plum, fig, and date.

It makes my mouth water to think of these desserts, and yet, what could be more delicious after a nice dinner than a bowl of cold fresh fruits—plums, apricots, peaches, strawberries, grapes, and melons of all sorts? So, although I am going to give recipes for several typical Armenian desserts, I advise you to make a habit of serving fruits.

The first recipe here is of very humble origin. It is called Imrig Halva, and is prepared with farina or Cream of Wheat. I was one of the many millions who, after the last war, were caught in the south of Russia where people were starving by the thousands. The world had forgotten that people in this section of the world had no food—all but the Americans. They came to our rescue.

At that time, I was working with the American Near East

Relief in the supply department. My specific job was to see that people got enough food to survive, and to see that the food was distributed evenly among the needy people. In one shipment we received tons of Cream of Wheat, with the recipe printed right on the package, telling us to boil it and serve it with cream and sugar. All very well, but we had no cream or sugar. And here it was, that tempting food, yet it wasn't palatable just boiled. So again the ingenuity of an old historic race was aroused, and the result was a beautiful dessert, Imrig Halva.

IMRIG HALVA

½ cupful butter

2 cupfuls farina or Cream of Wheat

3 cupfuls simple syrup or diluted honey (1 cupful
   honey or sugar to 2 cups water)

¼ cupful pine nuts (optional)

Melt butter; add farina or Cream of Wheat and pine nuts. Braise well, stirring constantly to prevent burning. When light brown, add hot syrup. Beat with a wire whip so that no lumps form. Pour into a buttered baking dish, cover, and bake for 35 minutes at 400 degrees. Take out of oven, stir well, and bake for another 10 minutes. Serve hot or cold.

PLUM PUDDING

For ceremonial dinners in America, we often serve plum pudding. It is our standard holiday dessert. And when you consider the amount of work involved in making it, it deserves to be a holiday dessert. I wonder how many realize that Englishmen have glorified this fine pudding by calling it English Plum Pudding. This dessert, however, originated in Corinth where currants and raisins were first grown. And mixing beef suet with desserts is an old Greek custom. Again we can trace national or racial similarities through foods—who knows but that some of the present residents of the British Isles are descendants of Caucasian or Greek immigrants who migrated there ages back.

Plum pudding is made as follows:

1 cupful beef suet
1 cupful butter
½ pound flour
½ pound seedless raisins
½ pound currants
1½ ounces lemon juice
5 ounces lemon and orange peel sliced thin
6 ounces brown sugar
5 eggs
4 ounces breadcrumbs
1 teaspoonful salt
4 ounces chopped nuts (hazel, walnut, brazil, pecan, or almond)
1 ounce cinnamon
1 ounce nutmeg
½ ounce allspice
1 cupful rum or 2 cupfuls sherry

Chop suet fine. Sift flour with salt and spices and add by degrees to the suet, mixing well. Now stir in all other ingredients, including well-beaten eggs, melted butter, and liquor. Grease well a square of muslin, and sift flour over it. Turn the mixture out on it, and tie corners of the cloth together to form a bag. Plunge this into a pot of boiling water which has a plate on the bottom. This will prevent the bag from sticking to.the bottom. Boil slowly for at least 4 hours.

Remove pudding from bag, and place it on a large plate. Sprinkle with sugar, and pour rum over it. Light with a match, and it will burn with a blue flame. Serve either plain or with your favorite plum pudding sauce.

EKMEK KHADAYIFF WITH KAYMAK

The *pièce de résistance* of all my desserts, which was originally made famous by my devoted friend, the late O. O. McIntyre, and then publicized by Rudy Vallee, is called Ekmek Khadayiff with Kaymak. Most everyone thinks it is my own recipe. But it is the creation of the famous chef, Tocatlian, who had the honor of entertaining the Empress Eugénie. It was for her pleasure that this master chef created his "bubbles of cream kaymak." It has become one of the outstanding desserts of Constantinople.

It has become very popular in our restaurant, and our patrons try to guess what is in it. For the last twelve years I have served it to gourmets, royalty, home economists, and food specialists. We give them ten guesses, and to my knowledge no one has guessed what is in the pudding. Some say apples; others say figs, prunes, and every exotic fruit in the world. In the end I always have to tell them that it is only bread cooked with honey.

EKMEK KHADAYIFF

4 cupfuls water
juice of 2 lemons
1 pint honey
8 slices zweibach

Steam zweibach with lemon juice and water. When it has puffed out, put it in a flat, round pan. Pour honey over it, and bake in oven until golden brown. This will take about 45 minutes. Serve with

KAYMAK

Boil 1 quart whipping cream on a slow fire. With a ladle, lift out cream and pour back in until bubbles start rising. Keep this up from ½ to 1 hour—it depends upon your elbow grease how high the bubbles rise. Turn off the fire and let cream remain in warm place for 2 hours. Then set in the refrigerator for at least 8 hours. With a sharp knife, cut loose bubbles of cream that have risen and set. Roll up and remove from liquid. Slice and serve on top of Ekmek Khadayiff.

ROYAL ARMENIAN PUDDING

This is a rich but exceptionally delicate dessert.

¼ pound blanched almonds
¼ pound pine nuts
¼ pound blanched hazel nuts
¼ pound blanched walnuts
⅛ pound butter
1 quart milk
2 tablespoonfuls cornstarch
1 cupful sugar

Put blanched, mixed nuts through a food chopper. Then shake them through a coarse sieve. Retain one fourth of the nuts, the coarsely chopped ones, for the top of the pudding. Bring milk to a boil, and pour in rest of nuts. Let simmer for ½ hour, then add sugar and butter and cook for 10 minutes. Take off the fire. Dilute cornstarch in half cup of water, and pour into mixture. Stir quickly to keep it from lumping. Return to fire and cook for 10 minutes very slowly. Pour into glasses for individual servings. Serve with the following sauce:

½ cupful sugar
1 tablespoonful butter
1 egg white
1 cup crushed strawberries

Beat one half of the sugar with the butter, and one half with the white of egg. When egg is stiff, beat in butter mixture, and fold in the crushed strawberries. Keep in the refrigerator. When serving Royal Pudding, put a dab of the sauce on top of each glass, and sprinkle the top with the remaining chopped nuts.

GEORGE MARDIKIAN'S ALL-PURPOSE CAKE

2 cupfuls brown sugar
2 cupfuls all-purpose flour (sifted)
½ cupful butter

Blend above ingredients together as for pie by pinching the mixture with the fingers. Set aside half of this mixture for the bottom of the cake. To the other half add:

1 beaten egg
1 teaspoonful nutmeg
1 cupful sour cream (1 teaspoonful soda added)

Mix sour cream and baking soda; add beaten egg and nutmeg. Grease well a square pan (9 x 9 inches), or use rectangular pan. Put in the crumbly mixture that has been reserved, and spread evenly over the bottom of the pan. Then spread other mixture over this and sprinkle the top with chopped nuts and cinnamon.

Bake in a moderate oven at 350 degrees for about 40 minutes. Do not open the oven door during half hour while cake is baking. The cake will have a hard caramel base. This makes a delicious cake for afternoon tea, or for dessert with fruit.

HOT CAKES HAYASTAN

2 eggs
2 cupfuls milk
2 cupfuls flour
2 tablespoonfuls sugar
1 tablespoonful baking powder
1 tablespoonful oil
1 teaspoonful vanilla extract
½ teaspoonful salt

Break eggs in mixing bowl and beat well. Add milk and sugar and beat thoroughly. Sift flour, salt, and baking powder together and add to eggs and milk, along with oil and vanilla. Beat well until very smooth. Bake in very small cakes on a hot griddle. When batter has bubbled over the entire area, turn lightly with a spatula and bake other side. *Never* turn over again! These are delightful with kaymak (see recipe on page 142) and rose petal jam, or other favorite jelly or jam.

PAKLAVA

5 cupfuls (1½ pounds) unsifted flour (Gold Medal
    Kitchen Tested)
5 eggs
5 tablespoonfuls peanut oil
2 teaspoonfuls salt
¼ teaspoonful baking powder
¾ cupful lukewarm water
2 cupfuls walnuts, put through medium fine chopper
1½ cupfuls sifted cornstarch
2¼ cupfuls melted butter
2¼ cupfuls melted vegetable shortening (Snowdrift)

Mix flour, baking powder, and salt in mixing bowl; then add eggs and oil. Knead for 15 minutes, adding water a little at a time, and forcing dough from edges to center of bowl. Keep the hands slightly oiled while kneading.

Sift a little cornstarch on the breadboard and put the dough on it. Divide dough into 4 equal parts, make each into a long roll, and divide each of these into 5 equal parts. Form these into balls, set in oiled pan, and roll balls about until covered with oil to prevent the formation of a crust. Cover with a towel and a pan over it and let stand at least 2 hours.

Cover a level-topped table with an oilcloth cover 1¼ yards square. Sift cornstarch lightly over this, lay dough on it, and roll out dough with rolling pin to size of a dinner plate. Then work dough over a wooden rod ¾ inch thick and 1¼ yards long, pressing out the dough lightly with your hands until it completely covers the rod, and roll back and forth several times. To roll dough evenly, unroll it from rod away from you, then roll it onto rod again, starting from edge directly in front of you. Keep oilcloth sprinkled with sifted cornstarch to prevent dough from sticking during this process. When the roll is about 22 inches in diameter, fold it over 4 times and set aside, covering it with tea towel. Continue until 10 of the 20 balls are rolled and folded one on top of another beneath the towel.

Cutting and setting dough in pan: Do not oil pan. Open and spread out 5 of the folded pieces of dough, one on top of another. Set pan in the center of these, cut the dough around it and place each flat piece in the pan with all the cuttings. Repeat with 5 more sheets of dough, and sprinkle evenly with walnuts. Place the remaining sheets in the pan in the same way until all are disposed of, laying the last cuttings beneath the last square sheet. With a sharp knife cut the dough diagonally into 5 sections in both directions, to produce 30 diamond-shaped cakes. Let stand 2 hours.

Take 1½ pounds butter, sprinkle in ½ teaspoonful of flour and simmer on very low fire about 20 minutes until it forms a white foam. Skim off foam and pour butter into a saucepan carefully, so as not to disturb the salt that has settled at the bottom of the pan. This should make 2¼ cupfuls of melted butter. Add 2¼ cupfuls melted vegetable shortening (Snowdrift). This should be kept at searing point when the Paklava is being baked.

Baking: The oven should get very hot and then be turned down to 350 degrees. Pour the hot fat mixture over the dough, 1½ cupfuls at a time, particularly into the cut edges and around side of pan. Place in oven, bake 7 minutes, pour over it another 1½ cupfuls of fat mixture, turn oven down to 325 degrees for another 7 minutes. Pour in the remainder of the mixture, turn oven down to 300 and bake 21 minutes. Remove from oven, drain off through a fine sieve all fat possible, bake another 5 minutes, drain off remaining fat and set aside to cool. With each pouring off of fat the dough mixture will rise and turn pink, and the pastry will have a crisp flaky appearance.

To prepare a simple syrup: Take 1½ cupfuls water, 2 cupfuls sugar, ¼ cupful lemon juice and a thin slice of lemon, and cook together about ½ hour until the consistency of honey is reached. When ready to serve the Paklava, pour this syrup around the edge of the pan and between the cut pastry, with a few drops on top. The pastry will become soggy if allowed to stand too long in syrup.

INDEX